The Old Leather Man

A Driftless Connecticut Series Book

This book is a 2020 selection in the Driftless

Connecticut Series, for an outstanding book in

any field on a Connecticut topic or written by

a Connecticut author.

The Old Leather Man

HISTORICAL ACCOUNTS OF A

CONNECTICUT AND NEW YORK LEGEND

EDITED BY DAN W. DELUCA

With the editing assistance of and annotation

by DIONE LONGLEY

A Series of Historic Newspaper Articles,

1869–1889, Illustrated with Maps

and Photographs

WESLEYAN UNIVERSITY PRESS

Middletown, Connecticut

Wesleyan University Press,

Middletown, CT 06459

www.wesleyan.edu/wespress

Printed in the United States of America

10 9 8 7 6

The Driftless Connecticut Series is funded by

the Beatrice Fox Auerbach Foundation Fund

at the Hartford Foundation for Public Giving.

Library of Congress Cataloging-in-Publication Data

Deluca, Dan W.

The old leather man : historical accounts of a Connecticut

and New York legend / edited by Dan W. Deluca ; with the

editing assistance of and annotation by Dione Longley.

   p.   cm.—(Garnet books)

"A series of historic newspaper articles, 1869/1889,

illustrated with maps and photographs."

Includes bibliographical references and index.

ISBN 978-0-8195-6862-5 (cloth : alk. paper)

  1. Tramps—New England—History—Sources.

  2. New England—Social conditions—1865–1918.

  I. Longley, Dione.   II. Title.

HV4504.D45   2008

305.5′69—dc22

[B]   2008029053

Editor's Note

I have several goals: to rekindle interest in the Old Leather Man; to pass his story on to our children, grandchildren, and future researchers; to remove the identification "Jules Bourglay of Lyons, France" from his gravestone in the hope that this will encourage others to try and solve the mystery of who he actually was and where he actually came from; to compile a list of known artifacts and their locations; to collect photos, postcards, drawings, and paintings of the Old Leather Man, identifying where they were done and by whom; to work with others to compile a list of his caves/rock shelters and eating places; to compile newspaper articles, letters, and any other information concerning him; and to publish written accounts of the Leather Man spanning the years 1856–2008.

This is a massive undertaking. If you would like to help or have any relevant information, please contact me or your local historical society

Respectfully,

Dan W. DeLuca

danwdeluca@aol.com

This book is dedicated to all of the people

who helped the Old Leather Man make his

journey through life, and to all the Leather

Man researchers who came before me. A special

thank you to Allison Albee and Leroy W. Foote,

who kept the legend alive, and to a young lady

and her family who donated her heart so I may

live. I received a heart transplant at Hartford

Hospital on Thanksgiving Day, 1998.

Who was the Leather Man?

Occasionally, legend and reality unite in
the form of some remarkable soul who,
through peculiarity or chance, assumes a
role resembling the mythical characters we
read about in childhood's fairy tales.

The Leather Man was one of these.

—Allison Albee, 1937

Contents

Preface

If you lived in the village of Deep River, Connecticut, in 1885 and looked out your window, you might see an odd figure trudging down the road—a man dressed entirely in scraps of leather, with a bulky pack on his back and thick, clumsy boots on his feet. His head down, he might dart a furtive glance at you before turning his eyes back to the road, finally disappearing into the distance. In driving rain or sweltering heat, the man would appear every thirty-four days like clockwork, always from the same direction. If you called to him, he might grunt warily, but he would not speak.

The Old Leather Man was a mysterious, forlorn-looking character who appeared in Connecticut and New York State around 1856. He was a wanderer, constantly walking the country roads and railroad tracks, sleeping in caves, huts, or lean-to shelters. He made his curious garments from soft-tanned leather cut from the tops of discarded boots, which he stitched together with leather lacing. His long coat had pockets on the outside and the inside. Spruce wood, three quarters of an inch thick, formed the soles of his boots; stitches of thick wire joined the soles to the leather tops. A cap with a leather visor completed his costume. He carried a large leather pack on his back and a tin pail in his hand. In later years, he used a wooden staff.

From 1856 to about 1882, the Old Leather Man traveled between the Connecticut and Hudson Rivers, making trips to the Berkshires in Massachusetts, and perhaps going as far as Canada. About 1883, he started traveling his famous clockwise circuit—a regular route of 365 miles every 34 days—until he died on March 20, 1889.

In his day, he was the subject of intense speculation. He seldom spoke, even to those who befriended him. No one ever discovered his identity or the reason for his constant wandering.

"Old Leathery" was probably born in the 1830s, perhaps to a French Canadian family. As an adult, he stood five feet seven inches tall and weighed between 140 and 170 pounds. He had a high, commanding forehead, black hair with a short black beard, and dark blue-gray eyes. He appeared to understand both French and English. He had a strong knowledge of Indian lore, which he used to survive. Where he had one shelter, another was never far away, and water was always near as well. He tanned leather, preserved meat, apples, nuts, and berries, and kept small gardens at several locations. At railroad stations, post offices, and country stores the Leather Man picked up cigar and cigarette butts. He chewed the tobacco he found and smoked it in a crude pipe of his own making. By 1888 people noticed a cancerous growth on his lower lip, no doubt the result of his tobacco use.

In 1879 both Connecticut and New York passed "Tramp Laws" that ordered the imprisonment of transient men, vagrants, and beggars. The Old Leather Man was not exempt from these laws, yet his lack of aggression—he did not steal, confront, or molest—made people reluctant to arrest him. He would at times take what was freely offered him, particularly from people with whom he was familiar. Sometimes he even consented to pose for photographs, and at least twenty images of him exist today.

On March 24, 1889, the Old Leather Man was found dead in his cave on the George Dell Farm in Mount Pleasant, New York. At the inquest, the coroner identified him simply as the "Leather Man" and estimated his age at fifty years. It was determined that he died on March 20, 1889, from blood poisoning due to cancer. His place of birth and parentage were unknown.

His remains were removed to White & Dorsey's undertaking rooms, where many curious visitors viewed them. Nearby was the leather suit that gave him his name. He was buried in an unmarked grave in the potter's field at Sparta Cemetery in Ossining, New York. For sixty-four years, a pipe sticking out of the ground marked the wanderer's final resting place. In 1953 a stone monument engraved "Jules Bourglay" was placed on his grave. At the time, some historians thought that it was his name, but no one has ever been able to verify it. "Jules Bourglay" has been traced to a name fabricated by a Victorian-era writer of a fanciful, romantic tale, which claims the Old Leather Man was a Frenchman disappointed by love. The newspaper that published the story in 1884 later confirmed it as fiction, but the myth has never died and the tale has endured for over a century. Other names with which he has been connected are: Isaac Mossey, Rudolph or Randolph Mossey, and Zacharias Boveliat. The Old Leather Man has never been legally identified, and his real identity remains a mystery.

Who, then, was he? Where did he come from? Why did he dress in leather? How did he survive? Why did he walk his solitary circuit through Connecticut and New York for decades?

Trying to find answers to these questions, I made many trips across Connecticut and New York, stopping at libraries and historical societies to go through old files, examine miles of microfilm, and talk to local historians. I searched out old-timers in many towns and listened to the stories passed down in their families. Searching for Old Leather Man images and souvenirs, I attended memorabilia and postcard shows and combed eBay. Through the years, I have amassed twenty different Leather Man photographs, hundreds of newspaper articles, and boxes overflowing with other research materials.

Retracing the Leather Man's steps, I found myself back in time, walking the same path that many had walked before me: Jonathan Tillotson Clarke, Alexander Gordon Sr., Alexander Gordon Jr., William A. Gor-

don, Alfred E. Hammer, James F. Rodgers, Chauncey Hotchkiss, Isaac W. Beach, Lanning G. Roake, Allison Albee, Leroy W. Foote, Foster M. Johnson, L. Raymond Ryan, Nick Shoumatoff, Patricia E. Clyne, Bertram R. A. Smith, Edward McKeon Jr., and Steve Grant. They too wanted to separate fact from fiction and bring the Leather Man's true story to light.

In December of 2006, the son of Leather-Man researcher Leroy W. Foote, Wayne Foote, contacted me, and he gave me his father's collection. His father spent over thirty years researching and interviewing people who had seen the Leather Man. Now, with Wayne's and his father's help, we have available twenty different photographs of the Old Leather Man.

I have not tried to write the history of the Leather Man but only to compile and transcribe information that was written about him in his time. This book is not a complete record of that information but a deliberately selected group of newspaper articles, documents, and images to represent this extraordinary man.

By publishing some of my findings as a book, I hope to preserve this material for people like me who want to go back in time—to bring alive the Old Leather Man as he was while making his strange and mysterious journey through life.

Dan W. DeLuca

Mother Goose's "One Misty, Moisty Morning," 1785

One misty, moisty morning,
When cloudy was the weather,
I chanced to meet an old man
Clothed all in leather.
He began to compliment,
And I began to grin,
How do you do?
And how do you do?
And how do you do again?

Illustration from Little Mother Goose Rhyme Book.
Leroy F. Roberts collection, publisher unknown, early 1900s.

Part I 1869–1883

Port Chester Journal, Thursday, August 26, 1869

The Old Leather Man

A Frenchman, aged about 35 years, dressed entirely in leather, stripped from old boot legs, etc., and who carries a leather pack on his back and a tin pail in his hand, continually travels about the country, coming from the same direction and passing through the fields at a certain point. Curiosity led me recently to follow this strange being and I found he had a home under a shelving rock, in the woods, where he has also a good well of water and a well tilled garden, fenced in with bushes and poles and kept in good order, but his vegetables do not flourish satisfactorily, owing to the poor soil. We could but wish this poor creature success in his loneliness.

 Robinson Crusoe[1]

Port Chester Journal, Thursday, February 10, 1870

RYE

A Strange Character—The Old Leather Man Again

Editor Journal: I suppose that many of the readers of your valuable paper have heard of the "old leather man," who has for the last year or so been seen occasionally wandering around this and other neighborhoods, and who has established his winter quarters in a wood belonging to Mr. Joseph Park, and bordering the road running to White Plains, between Purchase and North Street.

 Hearing the reports about this singular recluse, I, in company with others, paid his haunts a visit. It is true, he was not at home to receive us, being, most likely, out on one of his recruiting expeditions; but we made bold to examine pretty freely into the arrangement of his

1. "Robinson Crusoe" was a pen name that Jonathan Tillotson Clarke used as correspondent for the *Port Chester Journal*, the *Deep River New Era*, and the *Connecticut Valley Advertiser*. An attorney, Clarke lived in both East Haddam, Connecticut, and his native town of Chester.

The Old Leather Man's cave/rock shelter in North Greenwich, Connecticut, 2005. Photo by Leroy F. Roberts.

primitive domicile. I had expected to find a sort of cavern, but such is not the case. A pile of huge boulders, in many places rent in twain by some great convulsion of nature and whose tops project several feet from their base, form no despicable shelter and under which this singular man, encased in leather, finds a temporary home. Near the base of this "rock-bound hill" is a small stream of water, which has been scooped out, forming a clear spring of no doubt excellent water, but, from the other surroundings, we were not tempted to taste. At the base of one of these boulders before spoken of, is erected a rude fire place for cooking purposes and removed some twenty feet, is what may be considered a sleeping room, a space of some ten feet square by two feet high. The ceiling is formed by a large slab of rock resting at each end upon others rocks, and being detached from the main body by a fissure of some two or three feet in width and which we observed was occasionally used as another place for fire, no doubt to warm the parlor or sleeping room on extra occasions. We also noticed several troughs of different lengths and dimensions, fashioned with considerable skill from the trunks of two noble chestnuts that had been felled for this and other purposes. These troughs were used as a receptacle for meat, hides, etc. Two were filled to completion with nauseous looking beef, another contained something which is not usually put down on our "bill of fare," and the largest contained a cow's hide immersed in ashes and water to removed the hair preparatory to tan-

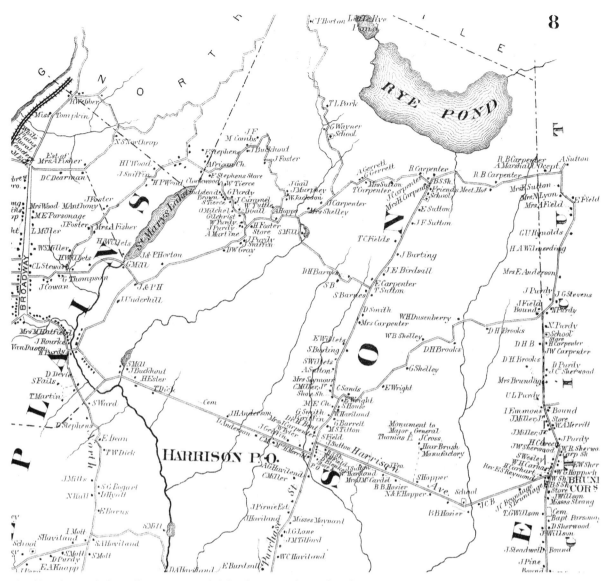

The Old Leather Man had one of his winter cave/rock shelters between Purchase and North Streets.
Map includes White Plains, Harrison, and Rye, New York. F. W. Beers, Atlas of New York and Vicinity, 1867.

ning and which, no doubt, is destined to replenish the dilapidated wardrobe of this eccentric individual. How or by what means this beef, (a large cow, no doubt) was obtained or conveyed to this place, remains a mystery. This together with the destruction of timber, caused Mr. Park to authorize one of his employees to watch and take him up for examination, but up to the present writing I have not learned that the feat has been accomplished. As this case is one that comes under the head of "tramps," it is hoped that, if the public has been injured by this prowler, he will be speedily removed to a fitting abode and the energies which he has already displayed be directed to a more useful and deserving purpose.

VINDEX.

Port Chester Journal, Thursday, February 17, 1870

Editor Journal: I notice in your last week's paper an account of the old Leather Man having a rude hut in Mr. Joseph Park's woods. I know Mr. Park very well and known him to be a gentleman of kindness of heart and liberal in his disposition and who would not disturb this poor, forsaken wanderer on any account if he understood his story.

The old Leather Man first made his appearance in this place [North Greenwich], three years ago this spring and since then he has been a constant passerby at least once a week until his presence has become a way-mark on the journey of life. He has always been civil and quiet in his manner and has certain houses where he calls for assistance and never stops at others along his route. Richard B. Carpenter, Joseph Griffin and Daniel M. Griffin are among the places he usually visits and like the good Samaritan they minister to his wants, never complaining of his coming too often. He has a rock in the woods on the east side of Byram River, where he makes his home when in this vicinity and there he has fenced in with poles and brushes a small garden. I visited his cave today and found it on the west side of a high rocky hill and under a large rock. The room is four feet high and six or eight feet square. There he has dug out two wooden troughs about four feet long and with covers neatly fitted to each. In one we found hickory

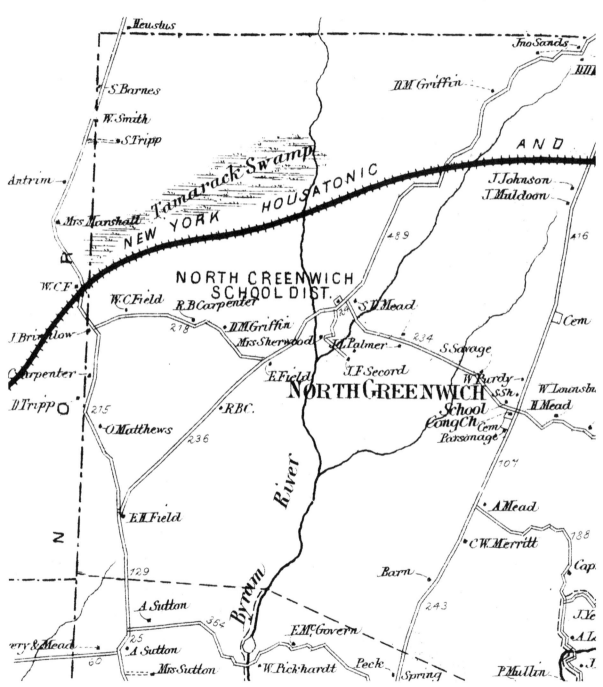

The Old Leather Man had two or more cave/rock shelters in North Greenwich, Connecticut. In the map, the home of Richard B. Carpenter is at center left; Joseph Griffin lived next door (right); and Daniel M. Griffin is at upper right. F. W. Beers, Atlas of New York and Vicinity, 1867.

Old Leather Man's cave/rock shelter; Byram River Gorge, Greenwich, Connecticut. Leroy W. Foote collection.

nuts and in the other scraps of meat, apples and pieces of beef hide, etc. There also was one of his shoes, the sole or bottom of which is made of wood and the tops of leather obtained from old boot legs, fastened by square staples of wire along the side, forming a very good and comfortable looking shoe. He has excavated under another large rock and made a cellar where he has stored apples, etc. that he has picked up along his way. In conversation with him we find he is a Frenchman and has been in this state about eleven years and cannot speak English and is undoubtedly a French Canadian. But why he has chosen this solitary hermit life we know not. His story may be a sad one and if we knew it, we might sympathize with him in his loneliness. But as it is, let us cast no shadows across his sunshine, but with kind words and acts may we soften his sorrow and make his burden no heavier for our coming in contact with him. I am confident, from three years acquaintance that no one need fear him in property or person. Make him no trouble and I am sure you will never regret it.

COM.

[With all due respect to our friend who penned the above, we must say we believe that the man referred to should be taken care of by the Poor Master and not permitted to haunt any community. His strange course of life may not thus far have led to petty thefts and other crimes, but is we believe calculated in the end to result in evil. The very food he eats, if his story is true, namely, the meat of cattle that have died of disease, must in time make him a most pitiable object, physi-

cally, and the life he leads is not calculated to improve, but contra wise, injure him mentally. He is either fit for the poor house or some other place. If one is permitted, aye! encouraged to live thus, how soon will it be before the woods in this vicinity are thronged with such miserable characters. We regard all such as tramps. They however roam in fixed localities, while their other brethren traverse the whole country. We repeat that the fellow should be taken care of at once. Here is a chance for missionary labor on the part of those who do not want the law to molest the Old Leather Man.—ED]

Connecticut Valley Advertiser, Saturday, December 27, 1873
CLINTON

The veritable "Old Leather Man" paid our village another visit last week. It has long been a query who he is, where he comes from, and where he stays nights. With the juveniles, the latter query is the most important, and for their gratification, more particularly we can inform them that his home is in a cave, in what is known as Elijah's ledges, in the west part of the town of Westbrook. In this lonely place he makes a home when he wanders this way. The cave is small and does not compare very favorably, either in size or gorgeousness, with the famous "Cave of the Winds" at Moodus. This queer specimen of humanity, clothed in leather, is indeed a curiosity. He is very reticent, only conversing when necessity compels it in soliciting food. It is not known where he came from, but it is generally supposed that he escaped from some Dime Novel.

The author, in 2005, at the Old Leather Man's cave/rock shelter at Elijah's Ledges (also called Lay's Ledges), in the western part of the town of Westbrook. Photo by Leroy F. Roberts.

Forestville, Connecticut; postcard, early 1900s. Leroy F. Roberts collection.

Bristol Press, Bristol, Connecticut, Thursday, October 29, 1874

FORESTVILLE

A "leather man" was recently seen in our streets dressed from head to foot in a cowhide suit. Every article of his gear, save his thick-soled sabots, which were rounded at the toes, was made of leather. One of the coldest nights of last winter he was seen under the mountain sitting near a huge rock by a fire, which he had kindled.[2] This singular being, whose nationality is unknown, converses with no one and wanders forlornly without a seeming motive, or definite object in life.

Connecticut Valley Advertiser, Saturday, April 3, 1875

Tramps

They are marching along the highways and the by-ways. Never was there a winter so prolific of these poor wrecks of humanity before. It has been a cruel season all over the length and breadth of the land. The cold, piercing winds, the deep snows, the chilling storms of rain and hail, and the long continued low temperature, have combined to make this winter one long to be remembered. Employment is hard to be obtained, in city or country; and many manufacturing establishments having been closed on account of dull times, it follows that hundreds, who have been trained to no other business, can find nothing to do. So they begin a wearisome tramp "over the hills and far away" to see if there may not be a realm of plenty somewhere—a distant El Dorado—which they may find by patient perseverance. They cheerfully journey along, unmindful of the biting frosts, or muddy, uneven roads, for hope ever cheers them on. Like the pilgrim of old, they each bear a burden—the burden of poverty and suffering. From some of them it will never be unloosed until they pass through the gate of death to the mystic land beyond. There, where every one receives his mead of joy or remorse, according to his deserts, many of these poor pariahs may, like Lazarus, be recompensed for the evils, which they endured in this life. Others there are, who are vagabonds from choice, or rather from lack of principle. They prowl around villages seeking what they may devour, and what portable articles they can appropriate to their own benefit. They have great faith and confidence in the generosity of their fellow-men, and never fail to test it to the utmost. Generally they travel by twos and threes. Rarely is one without a companion or "pal."

2. This rock shelter was located on the side of Red-Stone Hill in Plainville, Connecticut.

Taken all in all, the subject is a very sad one. It is melancholy to see so many lives which might have been made useful in their day and generation, so completely laid waste. The storms of Adversity are fiercer than the storms of winter; fearful are the shipwrecks, which are wrought by their relentless might.

There is one wanderer, often seen in these regions, over whose history hangs a mist which curiosity has never been able to penetrate. Summer and winter his costume consists of a suit of leather. He scorns the caprices and whims of Fashion, and, with a noble independence, pleases himself. But he evidently considers leather too light and gossamer-like a material to be made into shoes, for his feet are always encased in good, substantial, wooden slippers. He admires nothing, which is flimsy. Nothing but majestic solidity has an attraction for him. He has a kind of temporary residence in a forest, away from all human habitations. When weary of wandering, or possibly, homesick, he returns to this little hermitage at different lapses of time. There, under a lofty, overhanging ledge of massive rock, he cooks his solitary meal, *a la gipsy*, and then lies down to rest beneath its friendly shelter. He is peaceable and harmless, but in him is the instinct to see the world, or at least, some portion of it, and soon again he "moves on." The Israelite were compelled to wander forty years in the wilderness of sin. Is this poor waif paying the penalty for some transgression? Wise men say that naught is made in vain. Perhaps all these wanderers are working out some mission, which has been assigned to them, although it is hard for us to perceive what that can be. Infinitely wise is the Ruler of this earth. He noteth the fall of the sparrow. Will he not consider even these?

Haddam Ct., March 30th, 1875.

Connecticut Valley Advertiser, Saturday, June 5, 1875
DEEP RIVER[3]

The "Leather Man" with his knapsack and staff, last week again passed through our streets with his usual solemn stride and unwashed serious visage. Where does he come from? and where does he go to? and who is he? In the language of T. Hood, who was his father? Who was his mother? Has he a sister? Has he a brother, or

was there a dearer one still, and a nearer one, yes, than all other? I ax you.

T. Hood[4]

Bristol Press, Thursday, August 26, 1875

Tramp, Tramp, Tramp
There would appear to be no immediate prospect of abatement of the tramp nuisance. Rather, the tramp seems to have become ubiquitous and the growth of his order is only equaled by its capacity for villainy and "general cussedness." The few mild measures taken in some sections for the suppression of this dangerous class have proved wholly inoperative, thus far. How long the community at large will continue to bear the inflictions before resorting to a more vigorous and wholesome treatment is difficult to determine. From the way in which people permit themselves to be imposed upon and cowed into acquiescence with all that these rascals insolently demand, we should judge that this is a sort of tramps' millennium and is to be of indefinite duration. At any rate the tramps are increasing and with their multiplication, robbery, incendiarism, intimidation, rape and murder in like ratio become more and more common.

This tramp nuisance will continue just so long as people submit to it and no longer. The remedy is within reach. It is a simple remedy, easily applied. It may appear to some to be harsh, but if people would be rid of the evil, they must first make up their minds that harsh measures are the only ones that can be made effective. In the first place, stop feeding tramps. Secondly, let every man, woman and youth learn how to use a revolver and have one or more of these useful articles in every house, especially if in an isolated situation. Then whenever a tramp appears, peremptorily refuse him food or shelter and escort him off the premises at the muzzle of a cocked revolver and if he isn't easily scared and attempts force, shoot.

A trusty weapon in every house and a disposition to use it on very slight provocation, will do more to squelch this abomination than any other means possible to use. And when people drop their squeamishness and sickly philanthropy and all other classes of criminals with that promptness and fidelity which is

3. Deep River was part of Saybrook until 1947.

4. Thomas Hood.

possible only by taking the law into their own hands, the moral atmosphere will improve wonderfully and life, property and virtue will be properly respected.

soft-tanned cowhide. He had a shambling, rollicking gait, and with his thick-soled sabots, "his footsteps were loud in the withering leaves."

Bristol Press, **Thursday, November 25, 1875**
FORESTVILLE

That dark-complexioned, forlorn looking "Leather Man" who attracts so much attention by his annual excursions through this place, appeared last Saturday on the camp ground. His external gear was made entirely of

Connecticut Valley Advertiser, **Saturday, December 4, 1875**
ESSEX

The old veteran leather man passed through this place on Thursday last, and as usual, he stopped at the house of W. B. Starkey, on South Blood street, and partook of

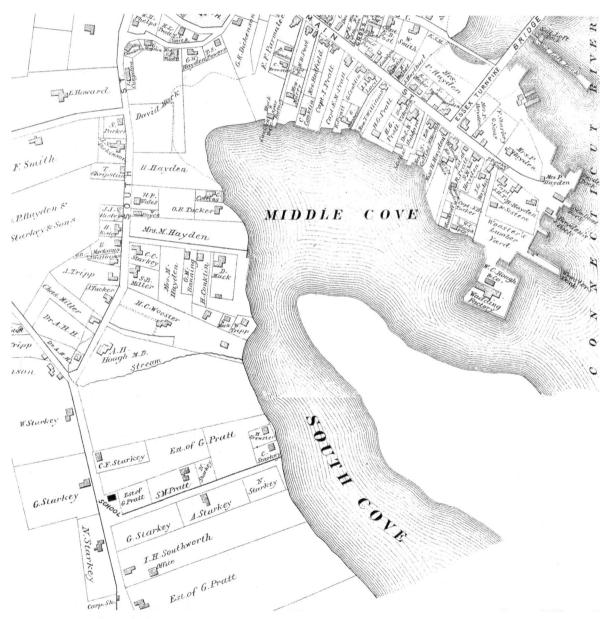

Essex, Connecticut: "Billie" Starkey lived in the house identified as "N. Starkey" (lower left).
Leroy F. Roberts collection, F. W. Beers, Atlas of Middlesex County, Connecticut, 1874.

Main Street, Deep River, Connecticut; postcard, early 1900s.

hot coffee, cake, pie, etc., as he has done for the past twenty years.[5] He makes his trips every six weeks. He is always on time and never fails.

Connecticut Valley Advertiser, Saturday, April 1, 1876

DEEP DIVER

The Leather man with knapsack and staff, last Friday, once more struck queerly upon our vision as with unwashed aspect and serious mien he passed silently by on Main Street, headed South, as he invariably heads in all his journeys through Deep River. We suppose there is but one "Leather Man" and him a revolver; if not, then we conclude there must be a large stock of them somewhere north of us, and also that by this time there must be a large lot of them south of us, for the "Leather man," or Leather Men, as the case may be, have traveled South through Deep River, at intervals more or less frequent for the last 20 years or so. We trust there is but one, because should so many leather men happen to concentrate in one place, it would be very confusing to the eye to pick out your own particular "Leather Man," and besides in a large quantity of leather men there

5. William B. "Billie" Starkey (c. 1819–1884) lived with his stepmother, Azubah Starkey, on the Middlesex Turnpike (now Route 154) in Essex. "South Blood street" is apparently an error.

might possibly be a good deal too much of a leathery smell.

Deep River New Era, Chester, Connecticut, Saturday, November 4, 1876

LOCAL RECORD

The "Leather Man" passed through our town last Saturday bound south. He looked natural and talked as lively as ever.

Port Chester Journal, Thursday, January 18, 1877

An Eccentric Wanderer

For fifteen or twenty years an odd looking genius, dressed from head to foot in leather, has made irregular journeys from this neighborhood to some place or places in the northern part of the county. Nobody knows who he is, where he comes from, where he goes, what his nationality is, or what is his age and name. He generally travels by unfrequented roads and whenever spoken to always pretends that he does not understand the language. We say pretends, because only a few days ago he met a young lady in a sleigh to Trumbull and asked her in very good English her destination and what were the contents of her sleigh. The suit he wears is

New Dug Way, North Woodbury, Connecticut; postcard, early 1900s.

always the same and apparently is made of bootlegs ripped open and coarsely sewed together. His boots are a wonderful accumulation of leather, one patch being fastened on the other till they are simply huge, unwieldy masses. His hat looks like a bootleg cut off and a top sewed in one end and a piece to serve as a fore-piece on the other. Everybody along the road knows him and the same title, "The Leather Man," is always given him. He gets his food by begging and always appears to have a first-class appetite. Taken altogether, he is a very singular combination and very many people would like to learn more of him. He sometimes comes along at intervals of a couple of weeks and then again will be absent for weeks and occasionally months.

Bridgeport (Conn.) Standard

Deep River New Era, Saturday, January 20, 1877
LOCALS

The old "Leather Man" passed through this place on Thursday calling at Mrs. Woodruff's[6] for food which

6. Harriet Woodruff lived with her daughter and son-in-law Louise and George Graham in Chester, Connecticut.

he ate, grunted his thanks and went on his way rejoicing. Who, and what he is; where he lives, and what are the causes that have conspired to make him what he is; are conundrums that throw all of Dundreary's "widdles" into the shade. He has a piercing black eye that denotes anything but a lack of intelligence, and his leather suit made up of old boot legs shows consider-

A 1937 newspaper article pictured Fred Barnes of North Woodbury at the entrance to the Old Leather Man's cave/rock shelter on the Barnes property, near Dug Way.

able ingenuity—enough at least to earn him a liveli-hood if directed into a proper channel.

Waterbury Daily American, Friday, February 9, 1877
WOODBURY

Several papers have made inquiries regarding an individual dressed in leather who tramps about from place to place. He is well known here, where he has a local habitation (a hut near the dug way between Woodbury and Watertown) but no name that we can learn. He comes over the hill from Roxbury way, goes through West Side and High street, avoiding the center. He is a mystery, and a very greasy and ill odored one, but considered harmless. We met him once in a lonely pass and had been of frailer sex should have dreaded such an unpleasant looking a being as he.

Waterbury Daily American, Thursday, March 1, 1877, Woodbury

Tramps are rather a used up thing, but the influx of them, since the extreme cold and deep snows have given back, is amazing. The other day there were ten able-bodied men lingering around the "slough" and whole families of the size of John Roger's though minus the latest infant, kept up a changing scene. I am told there are gypsies camped in a bend below us. The now widely known "leather man" passed through here last week. The paragraphs from the various newspapers so touchingly alluding to him had been preserved and were presented to him. He grunted over them, but showed no enthusiasm at finding himself famous in a single week. That he can read seems to be an open question.

Gypsy camp, late 1800s, North Main Street, Thomaston, Connecticut.
From North Woodbury the gypsies would go through Watertown to Thomaston, Connecticut.

Goshen Center

Goshen, Conn.

Goshen Center, Goshen, Connecticut, postcard early 1900s.

Woodbury Reporter, Thursday, April 1, 1877

A. & W. A. GORDON,

MANUFACTURERS OF

Fine Russet Leather,

For FOLDING REINS, SHOT
Bags, Suspenders, Saddle Bags,
Strapping; also Calf Skins & Splits.
Highest price paid for Calf Skins,
Hides & Bark. Hair & Lime for sale.
WOODBURY, CT.

Alexander and William A. Gordon owned the Gordon Tannery in Woodbury, Connecticut. The Gordons gave the Old Leather Man long strips of calf leather, which he used to lace together his suit.

Litchfield Enquirer, Thursday, June 14, 1877

GOSHEN NO. 291

Leather Man.—Your readers have heard of this singular man, but they have not all seen him. He passed through our place last week, and, like the Wandering Jew, there is something very mysterious about him. He has on shoes of leather, and his cap, coat and pants are made of boot legs curiously sewed with leather strings. He asked for something to eat, and he is not refused, for all wish to examine his clothes while he is eating. He expresses no thanks for food, and says little except "yes." If he would use a razor he would be a good looking man.

H.N.[7]

Woodbury Reporter, Thursday, December 13, 1877

To the Editor of the Reporter: Thinking your readers would like to know something about a mysterious char-

7. Henry Norton.

Alexander Gordon's House and Gordon's Tannery, Woodbury, Connecticut, 1877 (Main Street looking north from Spring Street). Courtesy of the Robert B. Cowles collection.

acter who travels through this place, I will give a short sketch of his birth. Twenty-five years ago the person known as the "Leather Man" lived in a thriving village in western New York. He carried on a large and profitable business as a tanner and currier, and was considered a prosperous and wealthy man. He owned a splendid mansion, beautiful grounds, horses, carriages and servants at command, and all of this world's goods the heart could desire. A sudden change came over him.

An incendiary fire destroyed his manufacturing establishment, together with his dwelling; the lady to whom he was engaged died about the same time. These combined losses unseated his reason, and he became a wanderer over earth, seeking for the loved and lost of his youth. Twice a year he visits her grave, covers it with flowers, and on his weary round he goes. Year after year he has held his way through summer's heat and winter's storm. Friends, speak kindly, gently to the old man. His sorrow was more than he could bear. The light of reason never to him will return, until he crosses the dark river to meet the friend of his youth, and loved and lost. Then will be rest for the weary one, the rest for all.

A.[8]

Waterbury Daily American, Thursday, January 17, 1878

WATERTOWN[9]

The "leather man" passed through our town a few days since. He does not ask alms at every house, and we wish that all tramps were as harmless and inoffensive as he.

Alexander Gordon Jr., August 1905. Photo courtesy of the Robert B. Cowles (great-great-grandson of Alexander Gordon Sr.) collection.

8. "A." was probably Alexander Gordon Jr., the Woodbury tanner who befriended the Old Leather Man. Gordon's accomplishments included arranging the American version of "Nearer, My God to Thee." He died in Woodbury in 1914 at the age of sixty-six.

9. The Old Leather Man had a cave/rock shelter called Black Rock Cave in Black Rock State Forest, east of Route 6 in Watertown.

Gordon's Tannery, Woodbury, Connecticut, 1877. Courtesy of the Robert B. Cowles collection.

Woodbury Reporter, Thursday, January 24, 1878

More About the "Leather Man"

Mr. Editor:—Your request for further information in regard to the "leather man" cannot be granted at present. His family are very reticent about his misfortunes. The friend who gave the information heretofore published in the REPORTER, is at her Western home, but expects to be with us in the Spring, when you shall have a continuance of the story, so far as can be given without betraying the confidence of a friend.

It is surprising how much interest is manifested by many in our village in regard to the sorrows and troubles of the poor wanderer-lonely, lost forever to his family and friends. Friends of the unfortunate: your kindness will meet return: in the "sweet by-and-by" when the dark river's passed your welcome shall be given.

A.

[If any of our readers are acquainted with any facts relative to his past history, we should be glad to hear from them on the subject.—ED.]

Litchfield Enquirer, Monday, April 8, 1878

GOSHEN

Leather Man.

This odd-looking mortal was around again, last week.

Litchfield Enquirer, Thursday, April 11, 1878

HARWINTON[10]

The "Leather Man" has begun his rounds again; he passed through the town, last Monday. He looks quite natural, except that the coat of dirt on his face is a little thicker.

10. The Old Leather Man had a cave/rock shelter near the intersection of Hill Road and Route 118 in Harwinton, Connecticut, known locally as "The Leatherman's Cave."

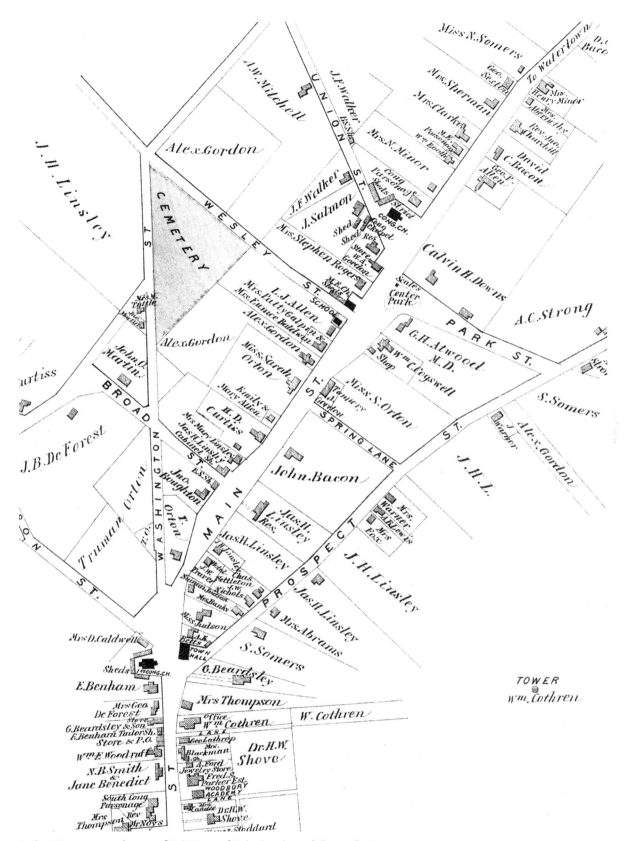

Gordon's Tannery was on the corner of Main Street and Spring Lane (center). Prospect Street was changed to High Street after 1874. F. W. Beers, Atlas of Litchfield County, Connecticut, 1874.

Litchfield Enquirer, Thursday, May 30, 1878

Leather Man.—This very singular being, like the Wandering Jew, has again made his appearance, and he still wears garments made entirely of boot-legs sewed together with leather strings. His cap is made of leather, and this year he carries a leather bag. As he walks his head hangs some lower than last year, and his countenance indicates that he has been doomed to walk up and down the earth for a thousand years.

H.N.

Litchfield Enquirer, Thursday, August 8, 1878

That strange and mysterious wight, the "Old Leather Man," passed through our village, last Saturday.

"I pass like night from land to land,
Like the Wandering Jew I never rest.
But an agony within ever urgeth me on."

Woodbury Reporter, Thursday, October 31, 1878

LOCAL AND OTHER NEWS

The "leatherman" passed through town on Saturday. We expect to receive a communication from "A." some time this season, which will interest the curious and all who care to know how and why the poor wanderer goes his weary round.

Port Chester Journal, Thursday, April 17, 1879

The Connecticut Tramp Law

The following is the Tramp Act recently passed by the Connecticut Legislature. We advise our readers to cut it out and keep it for reference:

AN ACT CONCERNING TRAMPS

Be it enacted by the Senate and House of Representatives in General Assembly convened:

SECTION 1. Every tramp shall be punished by imprisonment in the State Prison not more than one year.

SEC. 2. All transient persons who rove about from place to place begging and all vagrants living without labor, or visible means of support, who stroll over the country without lawful occasion, shall be held to be tramps within the meaning of this act.

SEC. 3. Any act of beggary or vagrancy by any person not a resident of this State, shall be *prima facie* evidence that the person committing the same is a tramp within the meaning of this act.

SEC. 4. Any tramp who shall willfully and mali-

Old Leather Man's cave/rock shelter on the Barnes property, North Woodbury, Connecticut. Leroy W. Foote collection.

ciously injure any person, which such offense is not now punishable by imprisonment in the State Prison, or shall be found carrying any firearm or other dangerous weapon, shall be punished by imprisonment in the State Prison not more than three years.

SEC. 5. Any sheriff, deputy sheriff, constable, special constable, or policeman, upon view of any offense described in this act, or on speedy information thereof, may without warrant apprehend the offender and take him before any competent authority for examination and on his conviction shall be entitled to a reward of five dollars therefore, to be paid by the State.

SEC. 6. All mayors, wardens and selectmen are empowered and required to appoint special constables whose duty it shall be to arrest and prosecute all tramps in their respective cities, boroughs and towns.

SEC. 7. This act shall not apply to any female or minor under the age of sixteen years, nor to any blind person, nor to any beggar roving within the limits of the town in which he resides.

SEC. 8. Upon the passage of this act, the Secretary of State shall cause to be printed durable copies of this act to be sent to the several Town Clerks, who shall cause the same to be posted in at least twelve conspicuous places, six of which shall be in the public highway.

SEC. 9. This act shall take effect on the 28th day of April, 1879.

Approved March 27, 1879.

Port Chester Journal, Thursday, May 22, 1879

The New York Tramp Law[11]

The following Tramp Law has just passed the New York Legislature. It is, with few unimportant alterations, the same as the Connecticut law:

SECTION 1. Every tramp shall be punished by imprisonment in the State Prison not more than one year.

SEC. 2. All transient persons who rove about from place to place begging and all vagrants living without labor, or visible means of support, who stroll over the country without lawful occasion, shall be held to be tramps within the meaning of this act.

SEC. 3. Any act of beggary or vagrancy by any person not a resident of this State, shall be *prima facie* evidence that the person committing the same is a tramp within the meaning of this act.

SEC. 4. Any tramp who shall willfully and maliciously injure any person, which such offense is not now punishable by imprisonment in the State Prison, or shall be found carrying any firearm or other dangerous weapon, shall be punished by imprisonment in the State Prison not more than two years.

SEC. 5. This act shall not apply to any female or minor under the age of sixteen years, nor to any blind person, nor to any beggar roving within the limits of the town in which he resides.

Approved March 27, 1879.

Deep River New Era, Friday, May 21, 1880

LOCAL ITEMS

The "Leather Man" passed through Deep River Thursday afternoon. His new spring suit is cut with a Basque and polonaise,[12] and trimmed with fourteen rows of boot-legs. It is said that the reason he is not indicted under the tramp law, is that he is a large holder of real estate, which he carries about with him.

Deep River New Era, Friday, November 26, 1880

CHESTER

The "Leather Man" passed through the village Wednesday noon. He wore his last year's ulster and looked a

---

11. Following the Civil War, thousands of men—many of them former soldiers—took to the road. In the army, they had discovered that there was a world beyond their own hometowns. They had also become used to long, forced marches (called "tramps"), periodic foraging for food, and riding the rails. When the United States entered an economic depression in 1873, thousands more found themselves unemployed and became transients, hopping rides on trains in groups. Some became belligerent in their panhandling. By 1879 both Connecticut and New York had established Tramp Laws that outlawed vagrant men. The Old Leather Man was not exempt from these laws, but because he was so well known by this time, few suggested actually apprehending him.

12. *Basque* and *polonaise* were nineteenth-century women's fashion terms. A basque was a tight-fitting bodice; a polonaise was an ornate overdress with a draped skirt.

little fagged, having been "on the slump" all through the late campaign. It has been ascertained that he is in company with Ben Butler, and the "old soldiers" he picks up are turned over to B.F.B. to be transformed into "union Hancock veterans." "Bernie" gave the old fellow a weed,[13] but if he thought to curry favors thereby, he missed it, for the Leather Man positively declined to be seen walking the street in his company afterwards.

Bridgeport Standard, Thursday, January 6, 1881

The "Leather Man," a peculiar figure that has traveled up and down the Newtown turnpike for years, has again made his appearance on that thoroughfare after an absence of several months.

Woodbury Reporter, Friday, January 14, 1881

For thirty years more or less, at nearly regular intervals, a mysterious character known as the "leather man" from his peculiar dress consisting of old boot legs ingeniously fastened together with leather strings, has passed through our town. Mr. Alexander Gordon,[14] with a view of learning something of his history, has frequently entertained him, also giving him on various occasions leather strings, old news papers, etc. Mr. Gordon has offered him money, but he always refuses to take it. A short time ago he in passing through the town called at Mr. Gordon's tannery, and he (Mr. G.) proposed to oil up his "clothing," which had become very dry and hard from exposure to the weather. As the "leather man" offered no objections, Mr. G. commenced business, using up two quarts of oil in the operation. Time was when he carried a large pack on his back, but he has substituted for that a leather bag, which is very heavy. He appears to comprehend all that is said to him, but seldom says a word in reply. In his journey through this village he always comes from the west, remains two nights within the limits of the town, always at the same places, in woods under shelving rocks.

13. Tobacco.

14. Alexander Gordon Sr. was born in 1814. At the age of eight he bound out (indentured himself) to David Stilson, a farmer in the Catswamp District (Roxbury). At the age of sixteen he became apprenticed to Deacon Elijah Sherman, learning the tanner's and currier's trades, and in 1838 or 1839 he succeeded Sherman in the business. He died in Woodbury, Connecticut, in 1893, at the age of seventy-nine.

In 1880 he passed through here ten times, or once in about 38 days. We are indebted to Mr. Gordon for the dates of his appearance, which are:

Date	Days Out
1880	
Monday, Jan. 19	—
Friday, February 27	39
Monday, April 5	38
Wednesday, May 12	38
Friday, June 18	37
Tuesday, July 27	39
Friday, September 3	38
Monday, October 11	38
Tuesday, November 16	36
Wednesday, December 22	36

His history would no doubt furnish capital for a romance, and if any of our exchanges or readers can throw any light on the mystery, which surrounds this peculiar character, we shall be pleased to have them do so.

Litchfield Enquirer, Thursday, November 3, 1881
PLYMOUTH SKETCHES NO. 413

On Saturday, the 29th, the "Leather Man" again passed this way; facing as is his wont, towards Harwinton. His most common day of arrival here is Sunday. He may have cut short his route a little, or, the weather being somewhat cooler, he may have gained a day on the same old route. On this occasion he is said to have partaken of a collation at the "Quiet House,"[15] the first time he has done so to my knowledge. There must be a last time that he will wend his way through our village, but it is hard to guess when that last time will come.

Plymouthean.

Oct. 30th, 1881

Woodbury Reporter, Friday, January 6, 1882

Mr. A. Gordon, Sr., has jotted down the dates of the appearance of the "Leather Man" during the year 1881,

15. The Quiet House was an inn and stagecoach stop.

Main Street, Chester, Connecticut; postcard, early 1900s.

Quiet House, Plymouth, Connecticut, early 1900s. Courtesy of the Plymouth Historical Society.

showing that he passed by his house on the following dates:

Date	Days out
1881	
Saturday, January 29	38
Tuesday, March 8	38
Friday, April 8	31
Thursday, May 12	34
Wednesday, June 15	34
Monday, July 18	33
Saturday, August 20	33
Friday, September 23	34
Thursday, October 27	34
Thursday, December 1	33

The longest time between his visits was 38 days, the shortest 31 and about the average, 33 days.

Litchfield Enquirer, Thursday, January 12, 1882
PLYMOUTH SKETCHES NO. 419

It used to be said that the "Leather Man" came along here once in every six weeks or thereabouts; but until recently I have paid no attention to the exact time it takes him to complete his circuit. Last Autumn I mentioned his coming through here on Saturday the 29th of October. His next appearance this way was on Saturday the 3d of December, precisely five weeks; and his next arrival Saturday the 7th of January, also exactly five weeks. According to this program we may expect him again the 11th of February. The weather changes do not appear to affect this "boss" of Connecticut tramps in the time it takes him to complete his "round!"

Plymouthean.
January 9th 1882

Date	Days Out
1881	
Saturday, October 29	33
Saturday, December 3	34
1882	
Saturday, January 7	34
Thursday, February 11	33

Reynolds Bridge, late 1800s.
Courtesy of the Plymouth Historical Society.

Woodbury Reporter, Friday, January 20, 1882
LOCAL INTELLIGENCE

It is now reported that the "Leather Man" once carried on a thriving and lucrative business in Poughkeepsie, N.Y., but trouble and disappointment made him a wanderer upon the face of the earth.

Waterbury Daily American, Wednesday, January 24, 1883
REYNOLDS BRIDGE

The leather man put in an appearance Sunday morning with an additional suit of old boot tops (perhaps a leather overcoat) under his arm. He took his old route up the hill to the east of the bridge. It is said that he has a stopping place on the hill to the east and a place on Plymouth hill where he always stops to get a cold bite. It is said, too, to be a peculiar trait of his to have regular stopping places on his route, hotels as it were, where he gets board and once in a while old boot tops to patch his pantaloons with. His language is small, for he rarely speaks to anyone.

Litchfield Enquirer, Thursday, March 1, 1883
ROXBURY

Leather Man.—This curious person passed through our village eastward bound on the 22d inst.[16] I met him about noon and asked him where he staid the night

16. *Inst.* stood for *instant*, meaning "this month."

Roxbury Station, Roxbury, Connecticut; postcard, early 1900s. Leroy F. Roberts collection.

before, "In the Woods." "Did you sleep there?" "Yes." "Were you not cold?" "Had a fire." I am curious to know if he ever in his routes finds lodging under a roof. His features indicate that he tells the truth, and yet one can hardly believe his story.

New Haven Daily Palladium, Friday, March 9, 1883

The Leather Man

For many years a very curious specimen of humanity has been traveling up and down the Newtown Turnpike and far beyond and he has been known all that time as the Leather Man. He looks tough and rugged, indicating that wandering life agrees with him. His great peculiarity is his dress, which is made so far as can be seen entirely of leather. It is a strange mixture of garments, if garments they can be called. They resemble nothing worn by anybody else in shape. They are made mostly of old bootlegs sewn coarsely but strongly together, some of them with leather strings. On his head he wears a sort of cap cut off squarely on the top and composed like the rest of his outfit, of leather. He generally carries a tin pail with him and begs at the houses along the route for food. Sometimes he puts the food in the pail and eats it as he goes along, and sometimes he sits down on the steps or piazza[17] and eats it there. He seldom speaks even when spoken to. For years he has

17. Piazza was a nineteenth-century term for porch.

made his appearance about once in so often coming south towards this city or going north towards the country. How far or just where he goes in either direction nobody seems to know. He made his appearance in Roxbury, February 22, bound east. In answer to questions he said in the woods the night before. When asked if he was not cold he said he had a fire. It is thought that he always sleeps out of doors.

New Haven Daily Palladium, Tuesday, March 13, 1883

LEETE'S ISLAND

In your issue of March 9, appears an article in regard to the "Leather Man" who travels in a mysterious manner through portions of Fairfield County. He has been well known in this vicinity for many years, but not until within the last three or four years has it been known that he was so methodical in his movements. He is always going west when he passes here, and it is always in the early part of the day. The preceding night he spends under a shelving rock in the woods between here and Guilford, and half a mile or more north of the railroad track. How he ever found this spot so remote from any road is as much a mystery as himself. He is usually gone thirty-four days, sometimes thirty-five in the winter season, and he has been known in fine weather to make the round trip in thirty-three days. His coming can be calculated with almost as much certainty as that of an

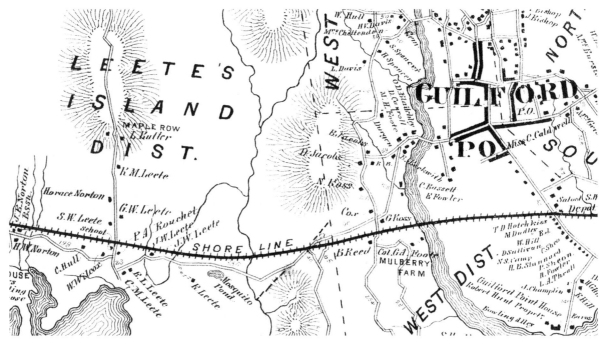

Leete's Island District and Guilford, Connecticut. The Old Leather Man's cave/rock shelter is in the west woods about a half-mile north of the railroad track between Leete's Island District and Guilford. F. W. Beers, Ellis, and Soule, Atlas of New Haven County, Connecticut, 1868.

eclipse, and with more than one of Vennor's storms or Wiggins' tidal wave. He passed there during the morning of March 6 and may be expected again about April 9, at nine o'clock in the morning. It is thought that his route for a few days previous to his appearance here is down the valley road from Middletown to Saybrook, and thence west along the Shore Line. After leaving he travels through Branford, and it is said spends the following night among the hills around Lake Saltonstall. Then he is heard of perambulating the towns of Fairfield County, and at the expiration of thirty-four days appears again from the eastward. He is an ugly looking customer, but is believed to be harmless. He never begs in this vicinity, and all attempts to interview him elicit only a grunt. What delusion he is laboring under, what his history has been and what impels him to this strange life are mysteries that have never been explained.

New Haven Daily Palladium,
Thursday, March 15, 1883
MADISON

More About the Leather Man—
The Hut Where He Lives
I have noticed in your paper several communications concerning the mysterious "leather man" whose strange

figure, and regular re-appearance and at stated intervals, have occasioned so much comment and curiosity throughout the towns where he has become a familiar visitant. It has been ascertained that this eccentric person, whose character and manner of life are unusual and interesting enough to warrant their perpetuation in the pages of romance, has for an abiding place a sort of hut built among the rocks about half way between Madison and Clinton. It is somewhat back from the road, not far from the railway, and for many years has constituted that dearest spot on earth, "home, sweet home," to this strange, silent wayfarer who has become a familiar sight along our highways. Here he lives when he is not journeying, which is presumably seldom, since, as your correspondence has informed you, his appearances are regular and unremitting. However, he has been found at home, sitting at the door of his hut, or cave, occupied in mending some old tins. Within were to be seen evidences of his domestic arrangements, which were not characterized by any undue luxury. As usual, to all interrogations and attempts to draw him into conversation, he presented the same immovable front, which for years he has maintained against the curiosity of the world with which he comes in contact. Whatever his secret is, it will die and be buried with its owner. Whatever malign influences have worked to create this strange individual life, whether he suffers

Old Leather Man's cave/rock shelter in Clinton, Connecticut. Photo by D. W. DeLuca, 2005.

from hereditary curse or carries in his heart the terrible history of undiscovered crime, will never be known. It would no doubt be both interesting and instructive could one trace out the long line of evil influences which have combined in his own early career, as well as in the lives of those who came before him, and resulted finally in this strange, weird, sorrowful life, over which hangs the veil of silence and mystery. It has been said that he does not beg, but there are however certain houses in our village where he never fails to stop, and where, although no word is spoken, he is sure of an ample meal and a kind welcome. Some day this incomprehensible character will fail to appear at his accustomed time, and somewhere on the weary roads or in the solitary, lonely hut, will doubtless be found the dead body of the queer old leather man, who from thenceforth will be to us but a tradition.

New Haven Daily Palladium, Thursday, March 29, 1883

ORANGE

That strange character, the "Leather Man," takes in the towns of Woodbridge and Orange in the regular course of his travels and was last seen passing through here March 9. He has been over this same route for many years, appearing regularly after an absence of about six weeks, always going south in the direction of Milford or Bridgeport. When in this vicinity he spends the night in an old barn standing along by the roadside. It has been his habit since the beginning of his travels through this region to stop for breakfast at the house of the writer, who had become so accustomed to his regular comings as to recognize his peculiar rap on the door, even when it was not known that he was near. Several

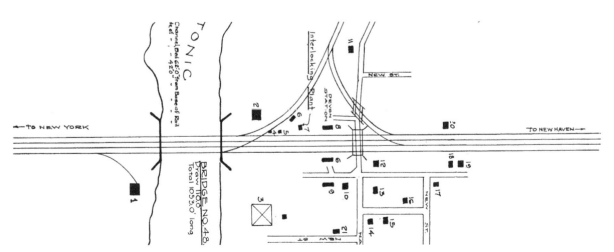

Naugatuck Junction, Milford, Connecticut. Leroy F. Roberts collection.

times attempts to enter into conversation with him were made, but with indifferent success, and on one occasion when we told him that "they had been writing about him in the papers" the information did not seem to interest him very much. However, since we have been the owner of a large dog who sometimes greets his appearance with a lusty bark he no longer stops at our door, but coolly trudges by on the other side without even deigning us a glance. Notwithstanding the little interest he evinces in the world and its goings on he has been seated by the road-side with a newspaper in his hands apparently deeply absorbed in its contents, and at another time, near a brook, washing some article of—we will not say underclothing, for that would spoil the tradition, but something that closely resembled it. Without his wonderful suit of leather he would be an object of curiosity, appearing as he does at regular intervals and always traveling in one direction. Whatever his aim or purpose, he trudges along as if he had the most important business in the world to perform, and as it was a matter of life and death that he should reach a certain destination at an appointed time. This strange creature's life in its unbroken silence, and stated goings and comings closely resembles that of the veritable "Wandering Jew."

Woodbury Reporter, Thursday, August 2, 1883

Mr. Wm. A. Gordon of Danbury, formerly of this place, is now local reporter for Danbury News.

The "leather man" astonished the Naugatuck railroad men on Wednesday by appearing at the junction and going toward Bridgeport. This is an entirely new field for him. *Waterbury American.*

Woodbury Reporter, Thursday, November 1, 1883

EDITORIAL MENTION

Mr. Alexander Gordon has kept an accurate record of the dates on which the peculiar individual known as the "Leather Man" passes through our town, and finds the average interval between his visits to be about 28 days. He has traveled through Connecticut and Massachusetts for a great many years, some of our middle aged citizens remembering him when they were boys, and

often recall the feelings of awe they experienced as they gazed upon his weird and uncanny person. Even to this day he is held in awe by the school-children as well as by some of the older people. He has had a habit for many years of stopping for food at the old homestead of the late Homer Root. It is related to us that not long ago he called there, and the foreign housekeeper spoke to him in her language (we think it was French) and received in reply in the same tongue a small portion of his strange history. He was a native of a foreign country, had met with great trouble and disappointment, and ever since had been a wanderer upon the face of the earth. He rarely refuses food, and never rejects proffered tobacco and cigars. He comes and goes, unmolested, unknown, but a true record of his life would form a tale more interesting than fiction—a record that will probably ever remain unwritten. He never seems to grow any older, his hair never seems tinged with a lighter gray, and his wonderful leather suit always reminds one of the past as well as of the present.

Deep River New Era, Friday, November 2, 1883

ESSEX

Below we give a description of the old "Leather Man" who has traveled through Connecticut and Massachusetts for many years. The old "Leather Man" has been traveling on the road through *Essex* once in every five weeks for the past twenty-five years and the only place he was ever known to stop for food is at the house of Uncle Billie Starkey, on Saybrook Street, and has never passed by in all these long years without stopping and has always been a welcome visitor at Uncle Bill's.

The Leather Man Interviewed

The New York Sun's Waterbury dispatch tells this story: For many years a peculiar person, known as the "Leather Man," has traveled through Connecticut and Massachusetts. Whence he comes and whither he goes, nobody knows; yet for at least a generation he has kept up his periodical peregrinations, appearing regularly every spring and fall. He is held in awe by some of the older people, many of them remember him as appearing exactly the same when they were young, and children are afraid of him. His apparel is of leather throughout, new patches being added from time to time. About all the figures known in trigonometry appear upon the coat and trousers, while his moccasins are decorated with triangles stitched with red string, trapezoids fringed with green yarn, and semi-circles done in cardinal. A slouched hat covers his head. Out from under this escape a few long, gray hairs, which are never any grayer, but are materially longer than when he first made his appearance. Upon his furrowed face is always a coarse, stubble beard, never any smoother, never any rougher, and his fingernails always preserve the same uncanny length. As he passes through a village, staff in hand, the school children shrink from him and older people wonder. "I remember well, when I was a boy," said a well known resident of this town, "meeting the Leather Man in the road as I was driving home my father's cows. Although forbidden by my mother ever to go near him, I did venture to address him. He gave me the only response he ever gives anybody, a stolid glance. Not discouraged, however, I asked him if he was hungry; a natural suggestion to a country lad; no reply. Still doubting, I beckoned him into the corncrib. Then I hastened to the pantry and returned with half a dozen doughnuts. Without a word he stretched his hand toward me and I placed the doughnuts beside him. He mumbled something, which I could not understand. Since then I have endeavored to follow him, but I could never see that he stopped anywhere for rest until this fall, when a day's journey was rewarded by seeing him steal into an outhouse at night. Pretending that it was an accident meeting, I joined him. He was engaged in scanning the well-thumbed pages of a small book by the light of a candle, which he carried with him.

"Well, old man, how are you?" I said.

Calmly he put up his book and started to leave. I put my hand upon his shoulder and stopped him.

"Whom have I the pleasure of addressing?" I asked with all due reverence.

"Ugh."

Ugh, and the old man shook like a leaf.

"Are you deaf?"

There was an almost imperceptible shake of the head and a heavy sigh.

"Tell me who you are!"

At this he started to take a yellow paper from his pocket, but suddenly thrust it back, as through recollecting himself. I offered him a silver dollar; he would not put his hand out for it. Baffled in every way, I had one recourse. I would trace him from day to day. I sent word immediately through the valley where his customary route lay to have intelligence sent me of his progress.

For weeks I traced him through Milford, Woodbury, Morris, Litchfield and up into the Berkshires, and back again to the vicinity of Norfolk, where all traces of him were lost in a piece of dense woods. A careful search of the woods revealed not a sign of a habitation and I am as much at a loss today to tell whence this strange creature comes, as are the many who have tried the experiment before. What is his life, what are the objects of his semiannual walking tours and how does he get his living, are questions that I should like to have answered.

Part II   1884–1885

Bristol Weekly Press, Thursday, March 27, 1884
FORESTVILLE

The "old leather man" passed through this village recently, headed south on the beaten track, which he has followed for the past 20 years. He was in possession of a large box, which it is presumed he intends to keep and use for a Christmas box.

Connecticut Valley Advertiser, Saturday, May 3, 1884
ESSEX

The old leather man, so called as he always dresses in a complete suit of leather, took his periodical tramp through this village last week. He has traveled through many of the Connecticut valley towns at regular intervals for the past twenty years, but as yet his name and nationality have not been discovered. His singular conduct has given rise to much comment, some declaring that he is the veritable Wandering Jew; others that he is Bret Hart's famous "Heathen Chinee."

Old Leather Man's cave/rock shelter, Westbrook, Connecticut; postcard, early 1900s.

Constitution, Middletown, Connecticut, Wednesday, May 27, 1884
STATE NEWS

The "Leather Man" has his abode in a cave in Westbrook about two miles from the center. When not on his travels he repairs to the cave, dreams and snores there, reads newspapers and cooks his victuals. He is generally absent from the village about six weeks at a time. Report says his name is Brown and that he has relatives in Hartford or the vicinity.

New York Times, Friday, August 15, 1884

That Leather Man Again
TRYING TO UNRAVEL THE
MYSTERY OF HIS WANDERINGS

Bridgeport, Conn., Aug. 14—Every few weeks the press of the State announces the sudden appearance and disappearance in some out-of-the-way locality of "The Leather Man." For the past quarter of a century this uncouth, repulsive, and wholly inexplicable person has loomed up in certain localities to puzzle the good people of those sections. Who he is and where he came from no one knows. He will not, if he can, speak to any one, and studiously avoids meeting any of his species. In the early part of this month Mrs. John R. Comstock, of Wilton, in this county, wrote a letter to the *Standard*, of this city, announcing that this uncouth and unkempt "What is it?" would appear at her house about *Aug. 13*. She based this assertion not upon any word received from him, but upon the fact that his visits to her house, where he has always been fed, were made at regularly recurring intervals. A record of these visits she has kept until she is satisfied of this fact. Sure enough, in accordance with her predictions, he did appear in Wilton on the very date specified.

Among the other places in this state, which this queer specimen visits with equally unvarying regularity, is the residence of a Mr. Hale, at the Naugatuck Railroad Junction, above Stratford. This point is four miles above this city and is 26 miles by rail from Wilton. The

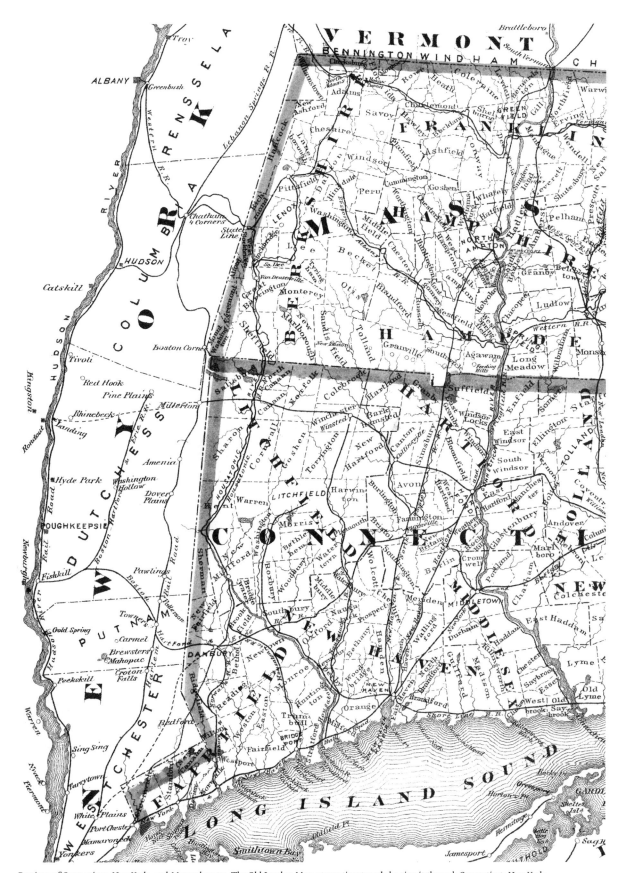

Portions of Connecticut, New York, and Massachusetts. The Old Leather Man at one time traveled a circuit through Connecticut, New York, and up into the Berkshires between the Connecticut and Hudson Rivers. F. W. Beers, Atlas of Middlesex County, Connecticut, 1874.

time taken by the itinerant from the Naugatuck Junction of Mrs. Comstock's is four days. What route he traverses is not known. It must be a circuitous one, however, for he always comes into Wilton from the northeast along the line of the Danbury and Norwalk Railroad. In this way he avoids the large cities, Bridgeport and Norwalk, and keeps in the farming districts. After leaving Wilton, he goes to a cave near the South Norwalk reservoir, about a mile west of Mrs. Comstock's, and then on toward New-Canaan. He also has a cave near Waterbury, in New Haven County, and another at a point between Bristol and Southington, in Hartford County, near Compounce Pond. The fact that he willingly visits the latter place leads those living near there to believe that he has a charm against attack from snakes, or else that he is rattlesnake proof, for the cave at Compounce Pond abounds with rattlers, which are so numerous as to prevent its being visited by the most

Old Leather Man's cave/rock shelter, New Canaan, Connecticut; postcard, early 1900s.

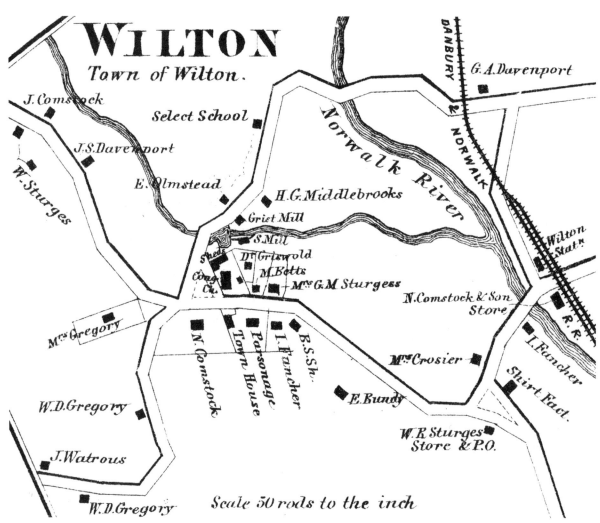

Wilton, Connecticut. F. W. Beers, Ellis, and Soule, Atlas of New York and Vicinity, 1867.

adventurous of the parties who daily visit that quaint and beautiful little spot. Some hold that the much patched and begrimed suit of leather clothing, which he always wears, is proof against the fangs of any serpent that might strike him.

Accounts published during the past 20 years show that the leather man has regularly visited Waterbury, Middlebury, Woodbury, Watertown, Southbury, Wolcott, Bristol, Oxford, Naugatuck, Bethlehem, Morris, Goshen, Litchfield, Torrington, Winchester, Newtown, Canaan, and other places in the northern and western portions of the state, with occasional visits to Rye, Mount Cisco, and other places in Westchester County, in New York State. These visits years ago used to be made at intervals of three or four months each. He would occasionally be heard from in the eastern part of New Haven County, and even in New London County. Visits to these last named sections have been abandoned of late years, however. In fact, the old tramp seems to have curtailed the district visited of late, confining his journeying to portions of Fairfield and New Haven counties, as nearly as can be ascertained. Within this territory his now familiar suit of leather, his leather haversack, wooden shoes, and the long, stout staff he always uses in walking are familiar objects once in five or six weeks. There is probably no one in the state who has been able to obtain from him any word in conversation, except the word "eat," which he uses and accompanies with a motion of the hand toward food. Those whom he regularly visits for his supplies are divided in their opinion as to whether he is French or Portuguese and as to whether he is sane or insane. There are disputed points between the farmers and their wives, which will probably never be settled. Linguists have tried him in vain when they could get hold of him, and have plied him with food and offers of tobacco and liquors. One of the most noted philologists in the State spoke to him in a half dozen different languages when he was once able to capture him in the town of Bristol. He could get no reply but a guttural sound which meant nothing, and which was more animal than human in its character.

Although there is in this state a severe law against tramps, making tramping a state prison offense, no one has ever attempted to put it in force as against him. The reason is that no one, women or child, fears him, for all know that he is a harmless creature, and tradition at least has it that he never did and never would harm anybody or anything. He has also an enviable reputation for honesty and sobriety. Concerted action seems now about to be taken to unravel the many years' mystery of his wandering, if not of his life. This bodes ill for the old man's peace of mind and some think will drive him out of the state to die, perhaps, in a strange territory.

Wilton, Connecticut, train station, where John R. Comstock was station master; postcard, early 1900s. Leroy F. Roberts Collection.

Waterbury Daily American,
Saturday, August 16, 1884

The Mystery Solved

By W. A. Sailson, Roxbury, Connecticut

THE ORIGIN OF THE ECCENTRIC LEATHER
MAN AND THE STORY OF HIS CAREER

The writer has noticed articles in different papers concerning that strange eccentric pedestrian called "The Leather Man," and as he has interested himself in finding out the past history of this strange character, he will endeavor to give to the readers of the AMERICAN a sketch of his past life, that has been gleaned from sources which will guarantee for its authenticity.

"The Leather Man" is of French parentage, and was born in France in the said old town of Lyons. Here his father, who was a wool merchant and in comfortable circumstances, gave him as good an education as the town afforded, and then sent him to Paris to complete it before going into business. Here Jules Bourglay, which is the name of this unfortunate man, became acquainted with a beautiful and highly accomplished young lady named Laron, the daughter of a wealthy leather merchant. He fell deeply in love with her at first sight, and as she returned his affection they became engaged before the parents were aware of their acquaintance. Her father was greatly incensed when he heard of his daughter's attachment. Jules, however, argued his case in so able and manly a manner as to soften the heart of the enraged parent in his favor, and the wealthy merchant offered to take Jules into his business for one year, and if he proved himself energetic and possessed of good business qualities, he was to have as a reward the hand of the daughter in marriage. On the other hand if he proved himself unworthy of trust he must give up all hope of gaining his suit and leave Paris never to return.

Jules agreed to these terms, and in the following week was installed in the office of his hoped for father-in-law, as confidential business agent. This was in '57, the year when leather fell 40 per cent. Jules had no inkling of this unforeseen danger, and thinking he saw a chance to add much to his employer's coffers, he speculated largely with a commodity that was eventually to drag him down to ruin and disgrace. Finally the crash came which involved so many in this particular branch of business and poor Jules, thrown out of employment, with the curses of his employer still ringing in his ears, was found by some good Samaritans wandering in the streets of the great city in a dazed and half crazed condition.

He was lodged and carefully cared for during the following three weeks, which he spent in raving delirium, calling on his loved one with endearing names, and cursing the ill luck that had thwarted his hopes of a bright and blissful future. The people who cared for the poor stranger so tenderly found the address of his father among some papers in his clothing, and immediately sent for the aged parent to come to his suffering son. This, the father did immediately, and as soon as nature permitted Jules was moved to his beautiful home on the Rhone. There, brooding over the unfortunate affair, his brain became weakened until he was a raving maniac.

Poor fellow! For two long years he was kept closely confined in a mad house. From there he finally escaped and came to America, where all trace of him was lost for three months. His relatives finally obtained information of his whereabouts and wrote to the New York authorities, giving his past history and telling them to spare no expense in finding out his condition both mentally and physically. This the authorities did. They found him traveling through Litchfield County of this state, as a traveling plumber, noted for his eccentric behavior, as he never took anything but food or tobacco for his work. His clothing was entirely of leather and he was said to have refused shelter, especially in a house, preferring the protection afforded by a barn, to the society of men. He was interviewed in North Canaan by Detective Walsh and found to be very reticent about his past history, merely giving his name and place of birth. He talked in a wandering manner, showing that he possessed a weakened mind, and when asked if he would "like to return to France," replied, "No, no," with a shudder of fear.

They informed his relatives that he was in a perfectly harmless condition and utterly abhorred the idea of returning to his native land. From that day to this nothing has been heard from them, but the Leather Man is constantly being heard from in newspaper stories, many of which have been exaggerated.

Afterward he forsook the plumbing business, and for 18 years he has been wandering around the country wearing his heavy suit of leather, as a penance, I suppose, for his disastrous failure in early life.

Nothing can be more pitiful than to see this poor, miserable, brokenhearted creature wandering around

William Augustus Gordon; August 1905.
Courtesy of Robert B. Cowles.

in cold and wet weather without even the common comforts of life, brooding over his terrible sorrow, which has cost him his happiness and prosperity. Treat him kindly, dear reader, wherever you meet him and lighten his heavy heart with acts and words of kindness.

W. A. Sailson,[1] Roxbury, Conn.

Derby Transcript, Wednesday, August 20, 1884

The Leather Man's History—
His Origin and Career

A ROMANTIC STORY WOVEN OF HIS PAST

A Roxbury writer to the Waterbury American claims to have looked up the history of the famous "Leather Man," whose wanderings through a portion of Con-

---

1. "W. A. Sailson" was probably a pen name of William A. Gordon, a reporter for the *Danbury News* and other papers. Along with his father, Alexander Gordon Sr., and brother, Alexander Jr., William owned Gordon's Tannery in Woodbury, Connecticut. In addition to his work as a tanner and writer, William A. Gordon served as financial agent for the Connecticut Temperance Union. He died in Danbury in 1909, aged fifty-nine.

necticut have been the subject of much comment and wonderment for twenty years or more past, and he has really succeeded in spinning quite a readable and romantic yarn. How he gained the information he now makes public is not stated, and it is questioned by some if he may not have drawn largely upon a vivid imagination for his sketch. It is certain the details given could not have been obtained from the man himself, as he talks to no one except in monosyllables, and what other research has been made is not stated. The story is a good one, however, and may be received with as much credulousness as the reader chooses.

Derby Transcript, Wednesday, September 3, 1884
WOODBURY

The "Leather Man" passed through here again on Saturday last. So much has been said of late, both wise and otherwise, in regard to this strange specimen of humanity, that one feels in duty bound to give him at least a passing notice. One who knows well his manner of life when at his cave here states that he is a great reader, eagerly seizing upon all newspapers offered him. Some years ago he used to while away some of his time in singing when at his woodland home, but of late nothing of this is heard. An attempt was made, though unsuccessfully, at one time, to get his photograph but he "had not time to stay."

Waterbury Daily Republican,
Friday, September 26, 1884
WOODBURY

Our hotels are still full to overflowing. The late fall of 50 deg. in the temperature did not frighten them away. That perennial humbug, the "leather man," engages the attention of several newspapers of late, and voluminous histories of him are given, which are just as good as any other, for the subject does not require any at all. He is not a tramp in the legal sense of the term, and does not bring himself within the penalties of the statutes. He never rents board or lodging, but goes on his solitary journey "saluting no man by the way," a veritable wandering Jew, finding nowhere rest for the sole of his foot. He is simply a nameless lunatic. He has followed substantially the same round year in and year out, for the last thirty years during which the writer has observed him, occupying some thirty days a little more or a little less, in his circuit, according to the state of the weather. He has many friends on his route, though he never talks with them, and will never sleep in any house. He has a little cave in the high rocks near Mr. Barnes' poorhouse, which he always occupies for the night as he passes through town. He has other set places throughout his route. A more harmless specimen of lunacy probably has never existed in this state.

New Haven Daily Palladium, Wednesday, December 31, 1884

The Leatherman

[By A. E. Hammer, of Branford.][2]

IN FOUR PARTS—PART I

Were one of the shades of Pluto's dreary realm permitted to revisit the earth and haunt our roads and byways, we might expect to discover the ill-omened visitor in some such guise as that which distinguishes the "Leatherman." Ahasuerus was no more a wanderer melancholy and solitary than this strange old man who year after year makes his unfriended way through our shoreline village. No record is there yet of word ever having passed his mouth; seemingly impervious to all human sympathy he continues his never ending tramp as isolated as he dwelt amid the wilds of some untenanted wilderness.

Along the dusty highways when the summer's sun seems scorching to death all nature's verdure with its suffocating heat, I have seen him with his suit of leather

2. Alfred Emil Hammer was twenty-nine when he penned a long, romantic fiction about the Old Leather Man. The New Haven Daily Palladium published the tale as a four-part serial between December 31, 1884, and January 6, 1885. A much-abridged version by Dione Longley appears here. Hammer, who had lived in Branford since boyhood, no doubt had seen his subject many times. His friend James F. Rodgers took several photographs of the Old Leather Man as well. By trade, Hammer was not a writer but a manufacturer, president of the Malleable Iron Fitting Company of Branford for many years. In creating his story—its flowery style characteristic of the Victorian period—Hammer drew upon his education in metallurgy and chemical engineering, and his interest in local rock formations. Hammer went on to serve in Connecticut's House of Representatives and Senate; he died in Branford in 1935.

and with pack on his back with panting breath and lagging limbs ever walking to the westward. The bitterest cold and the deepest snow of winter fail alike to check his determined progress. Sitting before the glowing fire snug within our wayside cottage, we look out upon the bleak and stormy reaches espying but one moving object swarthy and uncouth against the white snow—the Leatherman.

My sympathetic reader, have I piqued your curiosity to learn something more of this old leather covered tramp? If so, I promise you additional enlightenment, and my only concern is lest in my desire to do him justice, I may say somewhat that might make him trouble, and trouble enough has he experienced for one world.

In common with others I considered him an ordinary vagabond until one memorable winter morning. While going the rounds of my traps I was attracted by the shrill scream of a rabbit. This meant that bunny had been caught in the snare by the leg. Thinking to watch unobserved the creature's efforts to free himself, I approached cautiously and peered into the thicket. My astonishment gave way to indignation when I saw a man bending over the trap. In order that he might not deny the theft, I waited for him to get the rabbit in his possession, but imagine my amazement when, instead of dispatching, hunter like, the struggling victim, he gently smoothed the ruffled fur, tenderly touched the injured leg and then deliberately set it at liberty.

I broke through the thick underbrush and confronted the Leatherman. He made as if to steal away, but my accusation of attempted theft and threatening of harm if the offense was repeated, brought him to an abrupt halt. For a moment he stood motionless, with eyes cast down, then to my infinite surprise approached me, laid his hand upon my shoulder, and said in well chosen English and with scholarly accent: "I have no fear of you and your threats would fail to provoke me to speech did I not feel that an explanation is due. My apology for setting free your noble prey must be an admission of my weakness; I have within me an unlawful portion of what men call sentiment."

Before I could recover from my bewilderment the Leatherman had stolen away into the forest. For days I pondered the scene, striving in vain to reconcile therewith the low brow, matted hair, ugly features and small glittering eyes—eyes which looked as if staring from beneath a mask. Can it be, I thought, that he wears a mask?

Like yourself, patient readers, I became anxious to

know more of this old man who for so many years had maintained without surcease his solitude and his dumbness. If you should go to a certain house in North Branford, situated in the vicinity of the Twin Lakes, and enquire of the right person, you might hear the following story. It will be eleven years ago next September that this event occurred.

The night which followed this day brought with it such a darkness and such a wildness as makes children shudder at every gust of wind which rattles the windows. On a night like this came a quick loud knocking at the cottage door. An elderly woman lifted the latch to admit the caller. A little girl sobbing bitterly was thrust by an unseen hand into the doorway. Her crying ceased as a voice behind her said; "Good woman, God moves in a mysterious way. His way tonight lies through your heart. He places this orphaned child into your hands and charges you with its care. I am permitted to be of only secondary assistance to His purpose. Here, kind mother."

PART II

This little child has become a fair, thoughtful girl now, and has brought back to the good mother a thousand fold her kindness. Quite naturally you ask, gentle reader, "and does this young lady know nothing more of the Leatherman, if it be to him that she is indebted?" Possibly she may. Indeed, there are those who tell strange tales about having seen her familiarly conversing, along unfrequented roads, with a dirty, villainous looking tramp. But if you wish to learn more, why not call upon her some time when she is back from Vassar enjoying her vacation.

This would conclude my knowledge of the Leatherman, were it not for the fact that I myself am slightly dashed with the vagabond spirit, which at times becomes quite irresistible, and in humoring its whims I am led into the deepest woods. As far as I am aware the tract in Branford which goes by the name of Turkey Swamp is the most primeval wilderness in these parts.

I hope that you will be fortunate enough to follow the course which I took one winter afternoon. It was growing late, and as I wished to gain the open road before nightfall, I thought to shorten the distance by a crosscut. Even under the thick pines the snow had in some way gained entrance so as to cover the ground about an inch. When I came upon a spot two feet square, wholly bare of snow, I paused to satisfy myself as to the cause. No sign of any burrow was visible, and

the more I pressed my examination the greater became my perplexity. Finally I jumped up and down on the place to determine whether or not the ground beneath was solid. The hollow sound resulting convinced me that it was not, and I commenced digging down into the unfrozen pine needles.

In the space of twenty minutes I had completely uncovered what appeared to be a heavy plank door. It was some minutes before I raised the door, and when I did the indistinct view of several well-formed steps threw me into a state of tremendous excitement. At length, summoning all my courage, I descended the thirty steps. There was a rustic chair at the foot of the steps, and as I yet could distinguish nothing beyond a few feet I concluded to sit down and wait for my eyes to get accustomed to the darkness. No sooner had my weight rested upon the chair than I heard underneath a great rattling as if made by machinery. Soon I heard footsteps approaching. Finally a door opened beyond me, admitting such a glow of light as to leave me for a moment sightless. When I could see again I perceived, advancing toward me, the form of a man bearing in one hand a very brilliant light.

The face of this man was pallid as marble, the eyes were set in a glassy stare, the long hair only partly hid from sight a dry, bloodless neck, and the head sat rigid upon the body. On came the terrible being nor stopping until close beside my chair. There he deliberately got down upon his knees; his outstretched hand held a piece of paper. I took it and in so doing touched the stranger's hand. It was like that of a corpse.

Before I had time to open the paper the obsequious porter rose from his kneeling posture, made a motion for me to follow, and passed into the room from which he had come. Keeping close behind him I heard the door go to with a great slam. Another door opened ahead, through which went the porter, but before I could follow, this door shut before me and I was alone.

Thinking that the proprietor would soon return I availed myself of the opportunity to examine the room. What surprised me at first was the great strength and heaviness of timber which made the roof and sides. The doors likewise were simply massive and looked invincible. Several bearskins lay folded into the form of a bed in one corner. In the center were several large gas jets burning which gave off much heat but little light. I raised the lid of a green chest and was surprised to find it filled with hard tack and smoked beef. A large jug nearby was full of water. The little table in the corner was the only other article in the room save two chairs, but on that table were an ancient looking volume of Baxter's "Call to the Unconverted" and "Saints Everlasting Rest," a pouch of tobacco and a pipe. The idea gradually dawned upon me that this room was a prison and I a prisoner. As I was regretting the indiscretion which had led me alone into such a dungeon, I suddenly bethought myself of the paper, which the porter had given me. It was a note written in a clear, legible hand, and read as follows:

> Stranger, you have consulted your convenience alone in timing your visit to my abode and notwithstanding the fact that I am deeply sensible of the honor you do me, still I beg that you will allow me to appoint the time when it will please me to receive you. This pleasure I must deny myself until seven o'clock, P.M., January 14, 1875. Until that time make yourself comfortable in this my reception room.
>
> THE LEATHER MAN.

This was all, but considering that it yet lacked three days and three nights of that time it was enough. There was such a sublime sweetness in this little note, such mock courteousness, that it made me furious. I resolved to prepare for three days of serene quiet and to follow the injunction of the master by making myself as comfortable as possible.

At a little past seven o'clock January 14, I heard footsteps outside. Again there sounded the rattling of wires and the moving of machinery; and as before came the pale old man bearing the brilliant light in the same stiff manner. The doors opened before him as if by the intervention of some spiritual power. Soon the porter came back and following came the Leatherman. I noted as peculiar the fact that the porter had been as dumb to the master as to myself. Not a word had passed between them. When the Leatherman saw me he stopped. "You must excuse me while I shed my extra skin. You will find it more comfortable in the other room."

And in truth, I did, for so saying he opened the heavy door by touching some hidden spring and led the way into a well lighted room, furnished in a manner that betokened a well filled purse and a cultivated mind.

PART III

The carpet was the finest of Persian make. The furniture was so ornate with carving that every chair was a work of art. A malachite mantle of massive size supported several Venetian vases filled with giant ferns. The walls were covered with a kind of plush; fantastic scrolls of a deep golden color graced the whole. Upon this background hung several paintings of allegorical import. Two niches were occupied by Venus and Apollo. Several parts in the heavy curtains revealed the presence of a large library. Among the books upon the table beside me I could not help but notice a volume written by one Johnathan Brewster, an alchemist residing at New London, inscribed to J. Winthrop.

I had not until now noticed that the pale janitor occupied a farther corner, still holding the light with mien as stiff as stone and stare vacant and set as death. Now once my eyes rested upon him I could think of nothing else, and I became convinced I was gazing at a corpse which had been made to simulate some of the movements of life. But a soft step behind recalled attention. An old gentleman of very courtly bearing stood beside me.

"Although an uninvited guest," said he, "I may yet bid you an honest welcome, for to speak the truth, my enforced solitude and silence are at times irksome. Will you shake hands, young man?"

Of course I shook hands with him and made haste to inquire if he was the man dressed in leather who a few moments before quitted me.

"Yes," he replied, "I am the Leatherman, and no doubt you will now think me a base hypocrite for masking my face and affecting dumbness before men. I wear a mask that I may be avoided by men, and thus freed from the greater hypocrisy which society demands for its amicable maintenance. I am past the time of caring what kind of feelings I inspire in others."

I caught sight again of the pale gentleman in the corner. "Pray sir," I interrupted, "will you now ask the old gentleman yonder to sit down?"

The Leatherman, as I shall continue to call him, actually smiled as he answered: "John Calvin's theology does not permit him to sit down. But don't waste the least compassion upon him. He has been standing thus for thirty years and has got quite used to it."

Observing my perplexity he continued: "You know John Calvin was supposed to have been buried in the cemetery of the Plaine Palais, Geneva. Many years ago while in that city I learned that his body had never undergone burial but had been embalmed and was in the possession of a philosophical society. After a great deal

of trouble and expense I succeeded in gaining possession of it. I re-embalmed the body after a process of my
own which renders the flesh, nerves and muscles nearly
as flexible as in life. By connecting a number of the
nerves and muscles with a powerful galvanic current,
his body may be made to go through some very wonderfully lifelike motions."

The Leatherman was gradually putting off his con-
straint and I now became emboldened to ask if he
would tell me some of the circumstances which had resulted in moving him to live the strange, solitary life
he had. For some time he hesitated as if considering the
matter, then he said:

"Your request is no more than I expected. You are
right, my life has been a strange one, and," he added
mournfully, "a sad one, as every life must be that records a failure. When a boy I was of a sensitive and
rather morbid disposition. I learned easily and my abil-
ity in solving the test problems given by the teacher
raised unusual expectations for my future, which finally
resulted in my being sent to college. While studying
medicine, which profession I had determined to adopt,
I made the acquaintance of a gentleman who exercised
much influence over me. He was a man of splendid
genius, but I was not wise enough to know how sadly it
was misdirected. He was deeply learned in the Arabic
lore and in the false science of the mediaeval ages. But
the problem, which now absorbed his attention, was a
method of embalming which would preserve without
petrifying.

"Captivated by his enthusiasm and by his represen-
tations of vast wealth, which such a process would
command, I neglected entirely my medical studies and
devoted two whole years to this art. It was time lost; yet
we did attain to a perfection which had never been
dreamed of. My companion went to Europe to realize
immense riches and was to write for me to follow, but to
this day I have never seen or heard from him. The study
of medicine had become distasteful to me, and soon
after a friend induced me to undertaking with him a lit-
erary venture. It happened to receive the support of pro-
pitious circumstances and flourished. Although my active connection with it was long ago severed, to this day,
owing to the generosity of my early friend, I receive an
ample income.

"I found myself with considerable leisure time. One
day, while reclining under one of the trees of York Square
in New Haven, I observed approaching me a young lady

of great personal beauty. She stopped and asked me if
Mr. Rosewell resided in that vicinity. Being well acquainted in that neighborhood I assured her that no
person of that name resided there. She turned slowly,
with a disappointed look, and soon disappeared from
my view. A sweet face and pleasant voice haunted me.

"That evening I endeavored to dispel the impression
which the young lady had made upon me, but to no purpose. While laboriously pursuing some abstraction in
Descartes, her form would come before me, necessitat-
ing such continual retracing of steps that I occupied an
hour reading a page; and then when I was about to
felicitate myself upon having at last confined my freak-
ish imagination, who should smile her approval over
the top of the book but the girl whose face I had looked
up into? Next day, I found myself looking into every face
I passed. A whole week brought no change, and after a
fortnight had intervened I abandoned myself totally
and walked the streets hours upon hours searching for
the face, which had so easily broken through my oft-
boasted indifference to female charms, and made me its
worshipper. To find her now became my only passion.

"Walking down Chapel Street, scanning every female face one afternoon, I saw in the streetcar the object of my long search. I motioned the car to stop, and
as I stood there upon the platform I felt the first moment's equanimity I had known for months."

PART IV

"The young lady got off at Guilford and so did I. Remembering a friend residing in that place who had
often asked me to call, I made bold to inquire whether
she could tell me where Mr. M. lived. She recognized me
at once and replied, 'I can serve you better than you did
me at York Square. The gentleman you seek is my uncle;
I am going to his house myself.' Suffice it to say my high
expectations touching her worth were more than realized. Acquaintance ripened to intimacy and affection
which I soon found to be mutual. We were to be married
the coming fall.

"But a terrible calamity awaited me. A few days before the time appointed for my marriage my fiancé was
taken suddenly ill and died. The shock crazed me, and I
was told that so violent did I become when I heard the
dull thud of the earth upon the coffin that I was only restrained by force from leaping into the grave.

"That night I started from a dream in a state of joy-
ous excitement under the delusion that by some mys-

terious science or recondite art I had succeeded in infusing life into my dear Corinne's body. I could not exorcise the sensation made by the strange hallucination. May it not be possible, I thought, to restore her to life? Dressing hurriedly I ran to the houses of two of the town's desperate characters, offered them a large bounty for their aid and silence, conducted them to the grave, and in an hour's time we had the coffin in a cart.

"Living in a hut close by was an old hunter friend of mine. To his hut we made our solemn way. I paid the ruffians and bade them adieu before reaching Joe's hut, leaving the coffin beneath a low spreading pine. The hunter was at home and received me kindly, but in the morning when I told him what I had done, he refused to allow the coffin to cross his threshold. He assisted me, however, to place it in this cavern. I succeeded in the course of two days in the melancholy task of embalming and rescuing from decay the beautiful body of my beloved.

"Not long after this a rich relation died, be-questing to me a valuable estate, which I immediately sold and with part of the avails completed and furnished these commodious apartments. The carpenters and workmen who assisted me I hired from various cities, arranging their coming and going in the night time so that by no means could they again discover my habitations.

"The following five years I spent in Europe studying such sciences as led to no good. I visited all the renowned men, thinking possibly to come at something which would aid me in solving the mystery of life. Alchemists talked learnedly about 'confections,' 'mercurial winds,' 'quintessence' and 'elixirs.' Despairing of finding any real knowledge among men or books I returned to the solitude of this cavern and undertook to do that which must bring failure to all who try to solve the eternal mystery—the secret of life."

In the proceeding narrative the old man spoke as if relating the life of some other person. But now his demeanor changed to intense enthusiasm; his face glowed, his eyes became animated. I saw before me the enraptured earnestness of a monomaniac. In an adjoining room were stowed expensive implements and apparatus made in Europe. Experiment after experiment he detailed with an ardor and an understanding grand to inspiration. When he came to give me an account of his efforts to reach his end through the study of magnetism and electricity I was astounded by his results. His science had enabled him to embalm perfectly, and corpses were made to move and tremble by means of delicate connections made with the numerous nerves.

"Wonderful," I exclaimed for the hundredth time.

"Yes," answered the Leatherman, "but not life."

His final experiment consisted in making clear the forces which travel from the brain to the various parts of the body. This he did by connecting numerous hair wires with the nerves and muscles of an embalmed corpse and placing the other ends in contact with different parts of my brain.

"Now," explained the old man, "several connections are made between your brain and that body through which you can control some parts of the nervous and muscular system of those arms and legs. Now think as if to walk."

I did so and the legs of the lifeless body moved as if walking. I thought of moving my arms. The sensation passed from my brain into the proper channels and my thought was followed by movement of the arms.

"It is possible, you see," pursued the philosopher, "for one mind to control two bodies, but the initial impulse must emanate from the brain, and alas, the life principle of the brain is unfathomable. The muscular and nervous system of the body would do good service for several hundred years did not the brain wear out. According to the energy of the brain's action must be the movements of the body when all the connections are unimpaired. For several years I have supplied myself with extra force by artificial means and hence I still continue to trudge along with the apparent vigor of youth, but the moment I detach my artificial engine I feel the old man that I am."

After his long effort he leaned back in his chair, and with a faint smile he sank into a state of silent contemplation. Unable longer to restrain myself I asked the question which had been forming on my lips so many times: "Sir, you have accomplished results which if known to man would make your name famous and give to it enduring renown. Why have you persisted in your voluntary seclusion?"

The old man raised his head and answered softy yet firmly: "Young man, what to most men would have been but the sorrow of a year was to me an affliction for life. The only stimulus to all my scientific achievements was the thought of restoring just one body to life."

"But," said I, "did you never all this time make any effort to break away from your morbid state of mind?"

"Yes, often; but always to wander back to this place

where I could look upon the only thing of value to me in this wide world. During my studies it became necessary for me to take exercise, which I did with such regularity as to make me the object of much disagreeable curiosity. My leather garments were given me by a hunter whom I befriended in his last sickness and with the help of a few more patches they will last me through the little time I have to remain upon the earth. And now, my friend," continued he, "I have but one more disclosure to make in the story of my life—come."

He went slowly into an adjourning room, gorgeously furnished. Several brilliant lights surrounded a large table upon which lay decked in her wedding garments the body of the Leatherman's first and only love. If I might judge by looking at the face in death what beauty must have belonged to it in life, I would express it as that type of loveliness which artists strive to paint on canvas and fail. We stood gazing in silence for several moments. Suddenly the Leatherman took me by the arm and said: "Come, friend, you must now see what to a nature of my sensitiveness must have been the loss of the dear one who is there."

When I parted from this cave of death it was nearly noon of the fourth day following the evening I made the discovery of the trap door. Several times since I have met the strange old man in his cavern in the woods, and every new meeting seems to disclose the stored treasures of a mind such as men reverence.

To those that know the Leatherman of the street, it will be hard to harmonize the impression he must make in his dirty and uncouth garments with such a being as I have sketched here. I advise you, good reader, not to attempt such a reconciliation, because you will remain unsatisfied until you can prove his nature, but hear him talk you never will. To all but you who have been fortunate enough to read these words of mine, written out of a reverence for the poor old man whom I have learned to love, he will always be the vagabond Leatherman with his pack on back.

Waterbury Daily American, Friday, February 20, 1885

FORESTVILLE

The "Old Leather Man" stopped to dine with Isaac Beach, Thursday, on his regular monthly tour, and H. N. Gale of Bristol came down to shadow the singular specimen but

This is the first known photograph taken of the Old Leather Man. Photographer Herbert Nelson Gale of Bristol, Connecticut, took it on Thursday, February 19, 1885. "It was by strategy that his photograph was obtained by the instantaneous process, the camera being concealed by blankets hung on a line in Mr. Beach's yard, in Forestville. Mr. Beach handed him a plug of tobacco. The picture is his position as he slung his leather bag over his shoulders and received the tobacco, the other hand grasping his 'Alpine stock'" (account published in the Meriden Daily Republican, Saturday, May 16, 1885). Courtesy of the Hamden Historical Society.

succeeded in getting only an outline, as he was an hour later than usual. Next month Mr. Gale thinks he can get a good picture, as the animal always stops at a certain place. Quite a crowd gathered to see the old man and gave him many articles, some of which he wanted them to take back as he could not carry so much. His face appeared to have been frost-bitten on one side and he was much more broken-down than formerly. He was followed to ascertain something of his singular movements, but the result has not yet been learned.

Peekskill Blade, Monday, February 23, 1885

SHRUB OAK

CORRESPONDENCE OF THE BLADE.

FEBRUARY 22D, 1885

Owing to the heavy rains and severe weather week before last the "Leather Man" did not put in an appearance on his usual day and there was consequently considerable speculation as to his whereabouts. Thinking that perhaps he had perished with cold in his lonely cave in the Saw Mill Woods we visited that on Tuesday night. The moon was shining through the leafless branches with all its exquisite brilliancy and everything was quiet and motionless save the brook that went roaring and spattering over its rocky bed. The ruins of the old saw mill, which has long been deserted, stood like a faithful sentry guarding the crooked path that leads to the secluded headquarters of the old leather man. Arriving at our destination we found everything in readiness for the proprietor. The bed of dry leaves were in good order and were held in their place by several pieces of chestnut rail. Being satisfied that his leathership was not at home we came away. On the following day the leather man was seen going to the cave where he rested during the night, starting again on his route the next morning, seeming eager to make up for the time he had lost. When passing the grocery store, Mr. Darrow beckoned for him to come in. Contrary to his usual custom of shyness he entered the store and took a seat that was offered him near the stove. After eating some crackers and cheese he was asked several questions but would make no reply. Finally, Mr. Darrow said, "I am old, (writing his age upon a piece of paper and handing him the piece). How old are you?" The leather man took the lead pencil and wrote five figures of which the following is

15342

A FAC-SIMILE.

Mr. Darrow's Grocery Store, East Main Street, Shrub Oak, New York; postcard, early 1900s. Leroy W. Foote collection.

What he really meant by these rude figures now seems to be a great conundrum. Some think he meant to say, that he was born on the 15th day of the 3rd month 1842. Others think that he will be 42 years of age on the 15th of March, while others, whose minds are capable of conceiving vast ideas, claim that the leather man must be 15,342 years of age. At all events this is the first time anybody has been able to obtain a manuscript from him and he will soon be requested to write in young ladies' autograph albums.

L.[3]

Waterbury Daily Republican, Tuesday, February 24, 1885

The Leather Man

IMPROVED BY ADVERTISING—HOW
HE PASSED THROUGH FORESTVILLE

The leather man was seen in Forestville last week Thursday by an attaché of the *Hartford Post*, who found him surrounded by a host of villagers, but non-communicative, as usual. The recent advertising he received in the newspapers, "a rich Frenchman whose loved one died," "the inhabitant of a big and splendidly furnished cave," etc, etc, has stood him in good stead. His big ration bag is now full; he hardly ever has to ask for food; delicacies are thrust upon him—the romance of his life is so remarkable, you know. He is even given newspapers, upon the supposition that he can read, and frequently money is given him—what does he know of money?

> A simple child,
> That lightly draws its breath
> And feels its life in every limb
> What should it know of—money
> —Wordsworth, slightly altered

In person the leather man is rather short and thick set: apparently about 55 years of age, with a face as red as a beet. The suit he wears is still made of boot tops (easily procurable), which are united with leather lacings. At Thomaston[4] he was five minutes late, his Waterbury watch having played him false. In addition to all these interesting particulars he is said to be badly frostbitten.

3. Lanning G. Roake of Shrub Oak, New York.

4. The Old Leather Man's cave/rock shelter overlooks the Naugatuck River in Thomaston and is called Jericho Rock.

Evening News, Danbury, Connecticut, Thursday, February 26, 1885

The famous Leather man is reaping a rich reward from the great advertising he has recently secured in the newspapers. He was at Forestville a few days ago, frostbitten and uncommunicative, as usual. He was surrounded by village people. The papers have pictured him as "a rich Frenchman, whose loved one died," "The inhabitant of a big and splendidly furnished cave" and lots more off the same pieces, and his ration bag is full. He hardly ever has to ask for food, for delicacies are thrust upon him, and often the gift takes the form of money. The Waterbury Republican says he was five minutes late at Thomaston, his Waterbury watch having played him false.

Litchfield Enquirer, Thursday, April 2, 1885

PLYMOUTH SKETCHES NO. 461

The "Leather Man" pursued his rounds with almost astronomical regularity. At about noon on the 24th, he passed through the Center, to the north; as he had previously done many a time. By various newspapers I notice that this singular being is attracting a much wider attention than in former years. Some interesting accounts, or suppositions, have appeared concerning him; more especially that statement in regard to his French nativity, and his long lost loved one, from whom he was forever separated in this life by the force of unfortunate circumstances. The following little incident throws the merest ray of light on the subject. Some time since one of our women, who is near middle age, and whose features are, perhaps, rather French that otherwise, met this wanderer in close proximity to houses near the village. Whatever he may observe in passing along, he is seldom seen to turn his head. But in this instance he stopped, turned, and gazed intently on the individual before him. She, feeling somewhat scared, hastened away without waiting for further developments. The presumption is that her countenance recalled to his mind *some one* whom he had known a long, long time ago.

March 30th 1885
Plymouthean.

The corner of North and Main Streets, looking east, Plymouth Center, Connecticut; postcard, early 1900s.

·

Meriden Daily Republican, Saturday, May 16, 1885
MERIDEN AND VICINITY NEWS

The Leather Man's Home

"The Old Leather Man's" cave[5] was recently discovered about two miles south of Forestville by two boys named Joseph Green and Willie Bourne. Two sides of the cave are formed by rock, and the roof is made by poles braced against one wall, and the fireplace is located at the entrance. In this rude hut was found a small quantity of dried beef, a paper of snuff, and two newspapers which were recognized as articles given the old man last winter as he made his regular stop at the house of Isaac Beach; also a match safe given him in Forestville was found carefully tucked away, containing matches, and a pile of wood was in readiness for his return. The sole of an old boot was left, the upper having been used in making his haversack and unique suit of leather.

5. Located on the side of Red-Stone Hill in Plainville, Connecticut.

Efforts made last winter to photograph this curious specimen of humanity were finally successful, and this picture and cave are the only tangible traces that remain of his singular habits and appearance after his mysterious coming always at the same time in the day, at regular monthly intervals, and always going in the same direction. It was by strategy that his photograph was obtained by the instantaneous process, the camera being concealed by blankets hung on a line in Mr. Beach's yard, in Forestville. Mr. Beach handed him a plug of tobacco. The picture is his position as he slung his leather bag over his shoulders and received the tobacco, the other hand grasping his "Alpine stock."

Litchfield Enquirer, Thursday, May 28, 1885
GOSHEN NO. 708

The old Leather Man is still seen in the South part of the State, but he don't come up this way, lately.

HN.

New Haven Daily Palladium, Monday, June 1, 1885
AROUND THE STATE

James F. Rodgers of Branford has taken a photograph of the Leatherman.

Morning Journal and Courier, New Haven, Friday, June 5, 1885
STATE CORRESPONDENCE

BRANFORD

James Rodgers has on exhibition at the pharmacy some very good photographs of the "leather man."

Morning Journal and Courier, Wednesday, June 10, 1885
STATE CORRESPONDENCE

BRANFORD

The leather man passed through here to-day. Mr. Rodgers succeeded in taking some good views of him. June 9.

New Haven Evening Register, Thursday, June 11, 1885

A Night With The Leatherman

By James F. Rodgers[6]

[In presenting the above cut of the Old Leatherman, now famous throughout this section of Connecticut, the *Register* takes occasion to say the photograph from which it was made was not such as to enable the engraver to produce a first class work. The picture, however, conveys a correct idea of this strange person's appearance. When it is remembered that the old fellow has a horror of photographers, and indeed, of anyone who seeks information, the difficulty of getting a desirable photograph of him will be realized.]

6. James Francis Rodgers was a writer, artist, and amateur photographer. Sometime in May and on June 9, 1885, Rodgers took several photographs of the Old Leather Man while he stopped to eat at the home of Mary Chidsey in Branford, Connecticut. Rodgers was a friend of A. E. Hammer, who also wrote about the Old Leather Man in the preceding pages. Rodgers went on to art school in Boston but at age twenty-two fell victim to tuberculosis. He died in Branford on December 7, 1887, and was buried there at St. Mary's Cemetery.

The Robinson & Foote Pharmacy, also known as the Totoket Pharmacy, was the first drug store in Branford, Connecticut, and the only one until 1890. Courtesy of the Branford Historical Society.

The Old Leather Man, photographed at the Bradley Chidsey house in Branford, Connecticut, by James F. Rodgers, May 1885. Courtesy of the Branford Historical Society.

THE LEATHER MAN.

Woodcut of the Old Leather Man by an unknown artist, circa 1885.

A Night With The Leatherman

"Hear comes the leather man!" I hear the shout repeated a dozen times, and as I reach the window a bevy of children are scurrying for a neighboring yard, where some of their numbers are already ranged along the fence, and peering anxiously down the road at the strange, ungainly creature coming toward them. Who could resist the curiosity of seeing him? The temptation seizes me as of old, and I cannot forbear its influence. My palette and brushes are hurriedly laid aside, and I am soon amid the juvenile group and, like them, gazing intently on the coarse features and bent form of the leather man. As he passes I noted a keen, scowling look under the shadow of the high leather cap so characteristic of the old man upon his journey. I waited until he was a few rods father on, then started out after him. Soon he left the dusty highway for the shady protection of some adjacent maples, and shortly afterwards turned into a gateway leading up to the porch of a great white farmhouse. Here he paused a moment, then gently tapping the door with his staff, seated himself on a bench

to await the result. His knock did not remain long unanswered, for soon a quiet, motherly looking lady, who has attended to his summons for a quarter of a century, opened the door and looked pityingly on the wanderer as he placed his great rough hand upon his lips and muttered the words, "Eat, eat, eat!" Then disappearing, she returned laden with dishes, which had been thoughtfully laid aside for him. In silence he ate his meal: then placing the remainder in his bag and taking up his staff, he was again ready for the road.

As he saw me standing by the gate, closely observing him, he focused that piercing look full upon me. Almost involuntarily I shrank under the searching gaze, but again, summoning up my courage, I stepped out with him, and accompanied the strange man up the street.

At every window I saw faces directed toward him, I heard venders repeat his name and enter upon current gossip concerning him. Two dainty school misses stole cautious side looks at him, and whispered behind their books the often repeated query, "Who is the leather man?" The urchins abandoned their sport as he approached, and stood with grave wonder gazing upon his weather worn face. But seemingly all unconscious the old man plods on, hopelessly striving to finish the weary circuit of that relentless journey of his life. For nearly a mile I walked beside him, but he continued as silent as the stones in his pathway. At times he looked inquiringly at me, but in no other way deigned to acknowledge my presence. Finally, as we reached the summit of Plant's hill, I ventured to speak, and looking him full in the face, said, "Leathery, this is a hard life of yours."

He gradually lifted his eyes until they met mine, then in a faint, sad voice answered, "Yes, yes." "But," I continued, "Will you not tell me why you lead such a life?"

He stood still a moment, and looked absently at me, then slowly shook his head and went on. I saw it was useless to question him further, and stood watching him until he disappeared beyond the next hill top, then turning, retraced my steps, with his melancholy words ringing in my ear, and mind still more entangled in the mysterious life of the strange, silent man.

I have seen him trudging through the slush and blustering rain of early spring: unflagging under the scorching summer sun: unrelenting as the last phantom leaves of autumn fell about him and "chill November's surly blast" proclaimed the advent of winter: and I have caught glimpses of him veiled by the blinding snow, ever plodding on his apparently endless journey, which will only terminate at death's door. Clad throughout in coarse leather, which in bygone days creaked a merry accompaniment to his footsteps—the sunshine and storms of nearly thirty years, with his unrelenting tramp, has left it worn and tattered, and replaced its luster with accumulations of patches and dirt—cumbersome and uncouth, even repulsive in his appearance, seldom lifting his eyes from his path, and never uttering a syllable, he is indeed a fit subject for many stories concerning him.

Maiden ladies unanimously agree that the leather man has been disappointed in love, but shudder when they think who could ever have been infatuated, by so repulsive a being. Others ascribe his wandering, and adherence to silence, to those of a lunatic who despises humanity and seeks to gratify his unknown longing by these never ending journeys. Misers, whom the old man seems to know and avoid by instinct, say he has vast quantities of gold and jewels hidden away in the dark recesses of some cave. All are creations of the imagination, existing only in their author's mind. But the leather man is indeed an enigma of humanity rarely to be met with. None save the weird, subtle genius of Hawthorne could do him justice in romance, and Dickens, with his inimitable faculty of description, would have found in him a study, while Dore, with all his uncouth grotesqueness of imagery, has scarcely conceived a more repulsive being. To those who have seen him any description would be weak and impotent, but to the unacquainted reader it may not be amiss to endeavor to transcribe the picture my memory retains of him.

He is about the average height, through very compactly built. His thick, dark hair straggles from under the great leather cap in tangled confusion, and when closely examined the intermingled gray gives ample evidence of the burden of the years which the old man has upon him. His face recalls to my fancy Hawthorne's "Monk of the Catacombs," since only seeming to harden rather than change its countenance. It is swarthy, and nearly obscured by a short, coarse beard and overhanging eyebrows, in whose shadows lurk his keen gray eyes with a piercing glitter. His nose and mouth are well shaped though the other parts of the face somewhat destroy their symmetry. His leather garments, from which he takes the name of the leather man, are made up wholly of boot tops, which have been from time to time, patched and mended until scarcely a vestige of the

original texture remains visible. His shoes are not unlike those worn by the peasants of Norway and Sweden though far more cumbersome, over his shoulder he carries a large leather bag, and in his hand a hickory staff, surmounted by a wooden ball. Such is a faulty pen picture of this unknown man who for nearly thirty years has excited the curiosity of all, and who is now more than ever encircled in mystery.

On April 2, 1885, I saw him toiling up the road, bent under his burden, and hurried to the farmhouse with a firm resolution to try and entice him into conversation with me. I heard the same knock repeated, and listened to his trembling voice as he pronounced the word "Eat." As the lady turned to bring his food I went out and sat down beside him. He looked at me in an indifferent manner, but no sound escaped him.

"Leathery," I said, "Will you please tell me your name?"

"Yes," he answered. "It is E-zek."

I then asked him if he was tired, and again came that melancholy "Yes."

"Will you take these from me?" I continued, handing him some cigars. He bowed his head in acknowledgment and taking them placed them in an inner pocket. I then asked him if he spoke French, and another "yes" was my only reply; by this time his food was brought him and he immediately began to dispose of it in a manner that quite astonished me. A few weeks previous I had been to his cave on Saltonstall Ridge, which had been found by tracking the old man in the snow, and had taken there from a piece of his old leather suit with its canvas lacing, which had been carefully hidden in a crevice of the rock, I suddenly thought of this souvenir and dispatched "Bit" Lane to my house to get it. He was not long in returning; as he came up the path the old man darted a horrible scowl upon the unsuspecting "Bit" in a way that brought that individual to an abrupt stop. He had recognized the leather. Handing it to him, I asked him if he had ever seen it before. He carefully examined the stitching, and putting it in his bag answered, "Yes, that is mine."

"But, Leathery, you must give that to me," I said. "You do not need it." He took it from the bag and placed it in my hand, saying:

"Here."

"Do you wish to go back to France?" I began.

He shuddered perceptibly and answered, "No! No! No!"

I knew from the little I had seen that it was an easy matter to arouse his suspicious nature by questioning, and decided not to trouble him by other queries until he had known me better. All the time he had been endeavoring to satisfy what seemed to me to be a truly ravenous appetite. Slice after slice of bread disappeared, and huge blocks of meat went after them in rapid succession, and the manner in which he consumed his pie and cake reminded me of an expert magician disposing of his cards. Finally after two quarts of coffee had met the fate of the foregoing articles, he took up his bag and staff, and as I turned to leave him at the gate, he extended me his brawny hand, which I shook heartily, and felt at last that old Leathery had taken me into his confidence.

I awaited his next arrival with anxious expectation, and just thirty-two days afterward I saw him trudging up the road, his unwieldy garments creaking in harsh discord with the rasping shuffle of his clumsy shoes. I went out to him and was pleased to see he had not forgotten me, for he came forward with outstretched hand, and smiled when I shook it. "Come, Leathery, and have something to eat with me," I said, and pointed to my house. He shifted his bag to his shoulder and directed his cumbersome bulk towards the gate as I led the way.

His appearance was provokingly illustrative of a monster turtle, as he shambled up the garden a few steps, and then pausing, poked out his head around at me latching the gate, then went cautiously on. With a few alterations, nothing more aptly describes the picture of him than the old darkey song by which George H. Boughton so appropriately illustrates his delightful sketch of "William Grobbyus."

The head must be bowed and the back must be bent
Wherever Old Leathery goes.
A few more years and his troubles all will end,
In the place where the wooden nutmeg grows:
A few more years he must tote the weary load,
No matter it never can be light,
Then, proud world, good night.

I could not get him to enter the house, so telling him to sit down on the porch, went and brought him some food. He ate for a few minutes, but upon the appearance of two or three more upon the scene, manifested signs of uneasiness, and taking me by the arm pointed to-ward the great farmhouse.[7] I went with him, and I waited until he had eaten, then started up the road, walking beside him. He willingly answered the few questions, which my limited knowledge of French would allow me to put to him. I asked him where he was going, and he told me that "in a little time to his cave." Again he extended his hand, as at Plant's bridge he turned to leave the road, and said, "Adieu! I will see you again."

I hurried home, and after putting up a little lunch, and arousing the dormant ambition of my friend "Jock," we started for the leather man's cave. He had gone by way of the railroad and I knew it was customary for him to sit down and rest for some time. We took the Cherry Hill road and cut across Holley's farm, around by the head of Lake Saltonstall, and from thence over the ridge and reached the cave in early afternoon.

I called it a "cave," though in reality it is a hut. All along his route, at regular intervals, he has built these hovels, in which he passes one, or, if delayed by storm, and has a store of food, two nights. Hence the regularity of his coming is easily accounted for. In every town he has one or more places where he obtains food; this he carries to his caves, and, as he is an enormous eater, it seldom serves him for more than two meals. Therefore he must go on in order to obtain more. There are few callings which we attend to with more unfailing punctuality than our stomachs, and as Leathery has only that one calling, it is not to be wondered at that he attends strictly to it.

He has built the hovel I have mentioned of decayed butternut trees laid up slanting against a stick which rests upon a large boulder and the projecting limb of an ash, the hollow of the trunks being laid up, perhaps to carry off the rain. On the south side he has piled up brush and stones, the eastern protection being formed by the boulder itself. Within is a rude fireplace, always kept clean and ready for use, and in the nook and crannies of the great rock his few accessories are carefully hidden and covered with leaves. A large flat stone, laid near the fireplace, is worn quite smooth, and around it are strewn a number of hemlock boughs, for his bed, the stone serving in the capacity of a pillow. Without a great quantity of wood ashes and embers have accumulated, showing that

7. The home of Mary Russell Harrison Chidsey, wife of Bradley Chidsey; she died in Branford in 1892 at the age of seventy-two.

he has tenanted his secluded hut for many years. The trees in the vicinity bear no evidence of his axe, as he never chops one down, but burns the old decayed wood, the hemlocks being the only exception, from which he cuts a few boughs for his bed. "Poor, homeless one, thy lot is indeed a hard one." I thought as I gazed on the wretched hovel, and the great pine above seemed to sigh in sympathy as the wind tossed its branches.

It was now nearing 3 o'clock, and every moment I expected to hear the crackle of the underbrush foretell the coming of the old man. We crept under the shadows of a clump of hemlocks and listened attentively for some sign of his approach. Half after three, four, five, but still no leather man. It was a cold, cheerless day, so characteristic of this lagging spring: trying to rain, and still not raining, the great smoky, ragged clouds chased each other over the ridge top in rapid succession, each one threatening to pour down a deluge of water upon us. The wind roared down the gorge and moaned among the trembling trees. Far below, the lake spread its ruffled surface into hazy distance, and Cherry Hill, away to the south, seemed twenty miles distant. At times, as the wind subsided for a moment, we heard the plaintive call of the chickadee, or listened to the clamor of the wind-blown crows as they shot over our heads in pursuit of some vagrant hawk.

Jock had a short black pipe and forgot all anxiety under its mollifying influences. He busied himself by replenishing this source of comfort, and building miniature mounds around the Ant Hills. He is a typical son of Erin, and when I told him of the dreaded snakes of "Pond Rock" and showed him its mottled boulders jutting out of the ridges some distance to the north of us, he held it in far more dread than the leather man.

I varied the monotony by going up to the ridge and looking off in the distant mountains or down at the quiet little village of Foxon, with its elm sprinkled meadow and undulating farms.

Half past 5! I crept hastily back and had just reached the friendly protection of the hemlocks, when I heard the long wished for crackling. Yes, without doubt, the leather man was coming, and if he possessed any nature, he would show it. I lay still as death and told Jock to do the same, and here many moments had elapsed, I saw through my screen of bough the well-known features of old Leathery. He came direct to the cave, carrying in his hand a black tin pail. When he reached the en-

trance he listened for what seemed to me to be twenty minutes, then threw down his bag, and put the pail inside. He drew a long breath as he seated himself on a rock and looked about him, and I confess I felt rather uncomfortable when I saw him put his hand round under his coat and, taking therefrom an axe, deliberately put his hand in on the other side and bring forth the handle. This he fitted into it, and after two or three raps upon a stone proceeded to chop a prostrate tree trunk into short pieces for his fire.

"Now, Jock," I said, "keep close to me," and slipped out from under my ambuscade. The old man heard the first crackle, which betrayed our presence, and in all my life I never beheld a person more surprised. He looked at Jock, then looked at my crutches and myself in utter astonishment, until I shouted, "Helloa Leathery!" Then, coming forward, he shook my hand heartily. I had Jock take the axe, which the old man rather reluctantly gave him, and proceed with the chopping.

"Now, Leathery," I said as he placed the great flat stone for me to sit on, "will you sit still?"

"Yes," he answered, and seated himself beside me, and, as I endeavored to transfer his rugged picture to my paper, I asked him these questions:

"How long have you been tramping?"

"Twenty-seven years," he answered in his broken English.

"How old are you?" I went on.

He muttered in a low voice, "Sixty-eight."

"And are you not tired?"

"No-o-o. I am sorry." As he dwelt upon the words I saw every limb tremble.

The Bradley Chidsey House, late 1800s. Here Mary Chidsey fed the Old Leather Man and James F. Rodgers photographed him. Courtesy of the Branford Historical Society.

"Sorry for what?" I queried. "What should you be sorry for?"

"For much. For much." He sighed and bent his head upon his hand.

"Will you tell me why you wear that leather suit?"

He slowly raised his head and mournfully repeated the words, "I don't know, but I am sorry."

"Did you make it?"

"Yes, a long time ago."

"But," I reasoned, "Why do you not throw it off, and live among your fellow men?"

"No! no! never!" The old man raised his voice and every nerve seemed strained to pronounce the words.

I did not break the silence that followed, but worked steadily on until the gathering dusk closed in about us.

He arose after awhile and bending over my shoulder looked down on the rude sketch I was making.

"Ah! From France," he said, as his wary eye caught

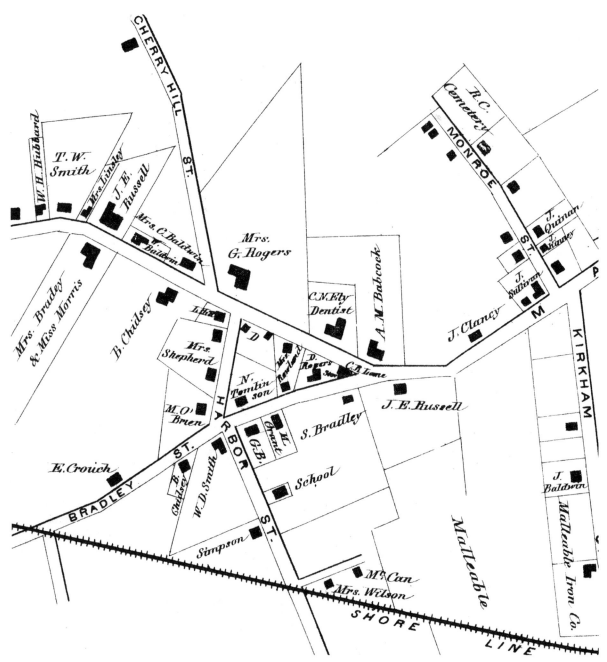

Branford, Connecticut: B. Chidsey (the Bradley Chidsey house, lower left), D. Rogers (home of Dennis Rodgers, father of James F. Rodgers, center), C. R. Lane ("Bit" Lane's house, next door right). F. W. Beers, Ellis, and Soule, *Atlas of New Haven County, Connecticut*, 1868.

THE OLD LEATHER MAN.

THE OLD LEATHER MAN.

The Old Leather Man, photographed on June 9, 1885,
by James F. Rodgers at the Bradley Chidsey house.

THE OLD LEATHER MAN.

sight of the crayon pencil in my hand, upon which was stamped some Parisian advertisement.

"Yes," I answered, though my conscience smote me for so doing, as I am confident the pencil was no more made in Paris than the rock I sat on.

He then went up to the old ash tree and rested his shoulder against it, and with his pitiful expression looked down at Jock as he sunk the axe deep into the fallen tree with every blow. No doubt he saw in the young man's stalwart form the counterpart of himself in years bygone, before age stole on, and he had learned the bitter experience of his lonely life. It had grown chilly, and I told Jock to light the fire, but the old man heard my request and hastened to comply. Soon the tiny match blaze caught the dry cedar branches and the dreary interior became radiant and cheerful. The leather man seated himself on a stone near me, and, as Jock filled his great pipe for him, I ventured to break the monotony.

"Leathery, are you not going to tell me something more?" I asked, and placed my hand upon his shoulder.

He reached his hand into a crevice and took therefrom a leather wallet, and untying the fastening, drew out a large paper and handed it to me. I unfolded it and, by the aid of the firelight, saw it was completely covered with curious characters, written in pencil and red chalk, and with scrupulous regularity.

"What are these?" I asked with surprise.

He waved his hand in a circle about his head, by which I concluded he meant his route, and these strange characters were indeed records of his journeys, for he took from the wallet sheet after sheet written in the same manner. I asked him for one which I held and he said, "Yes, keep it." He then took out another, though smaller wallet, which contained a pair of scissors, some thread, a bone comb, and a piece of cloth. He took the latter in his hand and slowly unwinding it disclosed a worn old French prayer book and a rosary which he reverentially bowed his head.

The thought flashed upon me:

He was a religious monomaniac living a life of terrible penance.

I became very eager to question him farther, and I am afraid he perceived my excitement, for when I asked him to tell me all about his life he sorrowfully shook his head and whispered:

"Not tonight, not tonight, but when you come again." Then, taking off his cap and kneeling down, he placed the crucifix in the crevice before him and opening his prayer book bent over the firelight.

I did not want to excite his ill will, and knew that he wished to be left alone, so taking his hand I bade him good night. Coming out into the darkness, we groped our way down the hillside and through the hemlocks, pausing only when we reached the open lot at the head of the lake. I could just see his fire, a mere speck, glimmering through the trees far, far up the ridge.

Poor, lonely wanderer, shivering over it when the

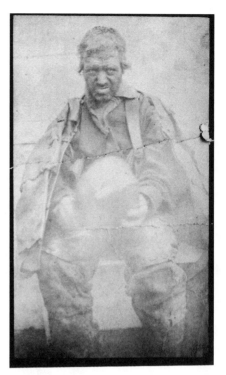

The Old Leather Man, photographed on June 9, 1885, by James F. Rodgers at the Bradley Chidsey house. Courtesy of the Branford Historical Society.

winter sighed and moaned about him, no companion, no home, naught but the sighing pines and silent stars of heaven. Years have come and gone and he has shared their sorrow, for with him pleasure is unknown. Let no taunting tongue molest him, for the leather man will soon be knowingly in "memories of the past and possibilities of the future." Should any of my readers visit his lonely hovel, let no sacrilegious hand be raised to hurry the crumbling pile to its destruction, for I look hopefully forward to the coming night when under its scanty shelter I shall see his dark features tinted by the fitful firelight, and hear him repeat in his low, sad voice:

"The Leather Man's Story."

Deep River New Era, Friday, June 12, 1885

CLINTON

The "leather man" passed through the town Monday and Eben[8] gave him a cigar. He makes his rounds once in thirty days.

8. During his stops in Clinton, the Old Leather Man visited Eben Buell's fish market and Harvey Buell's home, where he was given food.

The Old Leather Man

THE STRANGE LIFE OF AN OLD MAN
CLAD ENTIRELY IN LEATHER

ROAMING THE STATE FOR 27 YEARS
*Living in Huts, Harming Nothing
and Refusing Gifts of Charity*

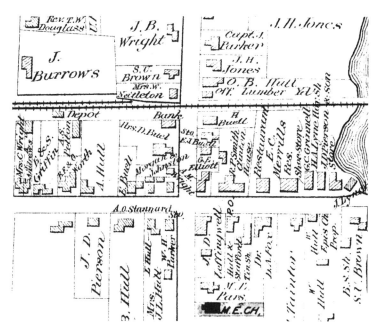

Main Street, Clinton, Connecticut; Eben Buell's fish market is at center left. F. W. Beers, Atlas of Middlesex County, Connecticut, 1874.

Detail of the circa 1885 woodcut of the Old Leather Man.

Above is the picture of a man whose peculiarities make him an object of curiosity and wonder to a large number of people in this state and some in New York State. For 27 years past he has come and gone over the same route, visiting each place with a regularity and preciseness which would lead one to suppose that he was traveling on an exact schedule of time laid out by him and from which he must never vary.

Very little is known about him. He is called the "Old Leather Man," a name he seems to accept as all that is necessary by which to designate him, and one evidently very appropriate, because his only visible raiment is of leather.

The Old Leather Man has been an object of curiosity as he passed on his regular trips at intervals of 34 days for the past 27 years and only fragments of his his-

tory have been written, but Chauncey L. Hotchkiss[9] of Forestville has for some years been corresponding with persons about the old man's mysterious pilgrimages until he has an account of nearly all his stopping places and many interesting facts concerning his singular life and habits. Stopping at one of his principal huts in the southeast part of Harwinton, Saturday night, July 4th, the old man—according to his time table, which is scarcely ever varied an hour—starting easterly about 10 o'clock Sunday morning and passing through the edge of Burlington, in Forestville at 2 p.m., and took dinner with I. W. Beach, a gentleman who takes much interest in the old man and is one of the few with whom "Old Leathery" converses.

When the strange pilgrim arrived in Forestville last Sunday, a considerable crowd had assembled to see him as he trudged along and some of the hoodlum element gave him so lively a reception that he was very glad to spy Mr. Hotchkiss to whom he hastily fled. So rough was the crowd toward the un-offensive old fellow that perhaps to prevent future annoyance he will after this avoid Forestville in the pilgrimage. After a 10 minutes stay at Mr. Beach's the old man struck out for one of his huts located in the woods near Southington. His

9. Chauncey L. Hotchkiss sold a large number of the Old Leather Man's photographs, and many newspapers printed engravings from the photos. Mr. Hotchkiss died in 1896 in Forestville at fifty-nine years of age.

direction from Southington; thence southwesterly is through Berlin, and the northern part of Meriden; through Middlefield, touching the corner of Middletown, Durham, striking the southeast corner of Haddam, where he turns south, traversing the river towns of Chester, Saybrook, Essex to the northwest corner of Old Saybrook.

Taking a course due west he passes through Westbrook, Killingworth, Clinton, Madison to Guilford. Here he has a hut built of railroad ties which he has carried up the mountain 100 rods, showing that he has the strength of two ordinary men. He makes this the stopping place for mending his clothing and general repairs and has been known to spend four days there. This time is made up on his trip into New York, as he was once nine days behind time at Wilton and arrived at New Fairfield on time.

From Guilford he proceeds to the northwest avoiding the city of New Haven by making a circuit through Branford, North Haven to Hamden, and thence southwest through Woodbridge, Orange, Milford, Stratford, northern portion of Bridgeport, Fairfield, Westport, Norwalk into New Canaan. Turning northwest into Wilton, he takes a westerly course into New York State, crossing the line near the Portsmouth and Ridgefield railroad. In New York State he touches Purdy station on the Harlem railroad, Kensico, Croton Falls, Doanesville and Southeast in the town of Brewster, eastern part of Peekskill, Yorktown and Shrub Oak plains. He has a cave in Turkey Mountains and Saw Mill Valley woods. He enters Connecticut from Southeast New York, near Ball's Pond, and pursues a northeast course through New Fairfield, New Milford, Bridgewater, Roxbury, Waterbury, Watertown, Thomaston and Plymouth and his hut in Harwinton, having made his circuitous journey which including the digression to reach his huts and caves (usually several miles from his direct route) is not less than 366 miles, 240 miles in Connecticut, occupying 22 days and 126 miles in New York during the remaining 12 days; but if through any cause he is delayed he shortens his trip in New York and is always on hand in Connecticut, so that Mr. Hotchkiss, who has correspondents in every town he visits, has prepared a complete time table of his travels. He stops in caves in Woodbury, New Canaan and Waterbury besides those mentioned above, but in other places his huts are built with rock and sticks leaned against them for a roof.

What little is known of him personally has been gathered in the same manner as his wanderings. Mr. Gordon, a tanner in Woodbury, once oiled his leather suit for him and they tried to have his picture taken, offering him some tobacco, but he refused. Mr. Nichols, postmaster in Woodbury, some years ago ascertained from him that he came from some place in France.

A gentleman[10] speaking French conversed with him recently and found he was 68 years old, a French Catholic and imagines that he is doing penance for some sin by such a life. He is about five feet eight inches in height, weighs 170 pounds and keeps his beard cut short with a pair of scissors, which he carries with him. His other belongings are a French prayer book printed in 1844, a tin pipe of his own make and big enough to contain a half of a paper of tobacco, an axe in one pocket and a helve in another long pocket in the back, a tin pail, iron spider, hatchet, jack-knife and an awl. Around his neck, underneath his leather clothing, he wears an agnus dei bearing a small crucifix.

He wears no underclothing excepting in the coldest weather and then only an old knit jacket. He seems to be interested in newspapers, and was seen reading one in his cave north of Woodbury. A gentleman in that vicinity met the Old Leather Man a short distance from home and gave him some pennies, but when he returned he found the same number of older looking ones on his horse block.

During one of the ice storms last winter he arrived at Mr. Hatch's in New Fairfield a little late and just at night. They tried in vain to persuade him to remain. They followed him to a piece of woods where they saw him gather up some sticks that he had apparently stood up there before, build a fire and settle down for the night.

He never begs and never returns thanks for what is given him. A lady[11] living near New Haven says that he has stopped there for 27 years. At this place June 9, several good photographs revealing distinctly his features and every wrinkle and stitch in his eccentric costume were secretly obtained[12] and from one of these the two pictures we present were taken. Mr. C. L. Hotchkiss of Forestville has more of them and will supply them at 50 cents each.

10. James F. Rodgers.
11. Mary Chidsey of Branford.
12. By Rodgers.

The circa 1885 woodcut of the Old Leather Man
appears again in a news publication.

Day	DATE	Time	Days Out
1883			
Sunday,	July 22,	2:45 P.M.	—
Saturday,	Aug. 25,	2:15 P.M.	34
Friday,	Sept. 28,	2:40 P.M.	34
Thursday,	Nov. 1,	3:15 P.M.	34
Wednesday,	Dec. 5,	2:45 P.M.	34
1884			
Tuesday,	Jan. 8,	2:20 P.M.	34
Monday,	Feb. 11,	2:35 P.M.	34
Sunday,	Mar. 16,	2:30 P.M.	34
Saturday,	Apr. 19,	1:55 P.M.	34
Friday,	May. 23,	1:55 P.M.	34
Thursday,	June 26,	3:35 P.M.	34
Wednesday,	July 30,	1:45 P.M.	34
Tuesday,	Sept. 2,	1:55 P.M.	34
Monday,	Oct. 6,	2:40 P.M.	34
Sunday,	Nov. 9,	2:15 P.M.	34
Saturday,	Dec. 13,	3:20 P.M.	34
1885			
Friday,	Jan. 16,	2:25 P.M.	34
Thursday,	Feb. 19,	3:20 P.M.	34
Wednesday,	Mar. 25,	2:15 P.M.	34
Tuesday,	Apr. 28,	3:05 P.M.	34
Monday,	June 1,	3:30 P.M.	34
Sunday,	July 5,	3:30 P.M.	34

Summer and winter the old man pursues his course with clock-like regularity, braving the storms of winter and the heat of summer. Quietly trudging his way, he asks nothing of anyone, does no act of wrong, but steadily plods along his way, doing penance for the wrong he did or supposed he did long years ago.

To city folks this old man may be of no remarkable interest further than that he presents one of life's phases totally different from any thing they see in their daily walks. But to the rural population and those through whose midst he passes so frequently with such great regularity, his peculiar dress, habits and unfathomable silence, is matter of unusual interest. Undoubtedly the old "Leather Man" is one of Connecticut's greatest curiosities.

The following table[13] shows exactly the day, hour and month at which old Leathery has passed the Forestville post office during the last two years. It is to be noted that at this end of the route he has not varied a day and in fact not over two hours.

13. The complete timetable was in the New Haven *Evening Register*, April 8, 1889.

We have another table of his passage west, past Naugatuck station. This varies a day or two, in one case three days, but since February he has made exact time, passing Naugatuck station each 34th day.

Deep River New Era, Friday, July 17, 1885
WESTBROOK

The old leather man passed through our village on Saturday last, bound west. The same day Crazy Margaret, another celebrity was in town.

Connecticut Valley Advertiser, Saturday, July 18, 1885

For heaven's sake let the "Old Leather Man" rest, or rather let him pursue his daily walk unmolested and without newspaper comments. Just so regular as this

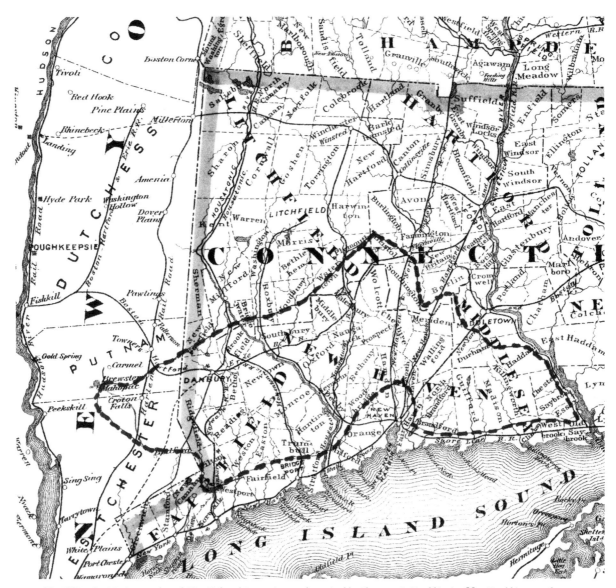

Map of the Old Leather Man's route through New York and Connecticut, as determined by Chauncey L. Hotchkiss in 1885. Hotchkiss started keeping track of the Old Leather Man in 1883 and also corresponded with others as he tried to trace his route. In 1885 Hotchkiss published his findings in the Hartford Globe; he had determined that the Old Leather Man traveled in a clockwise 366-mile circuit in thirty-four days between the Connecticut and Hudson Rivers. By 1883 the Old Leather Man had given up his northern and southern routes. From 1883 through 1889 even this route would vary at times, as he abandoned some places and added others. F. W. Beers, Atlas of Middlesex County, Connecticut, 1874.

old crank makes his rounds, just so often do newspapers reporters write up that he has passed through their town on such a day. The *Advertiser*, as well as the other papers in this county, has been called upon to make this important announcement too often.

Penny Press, Saturday, August 15, 1885

ESSEX

The "Leather Man" passed through this town yesterday. He stopped out at Mud River Bridge, and throwing his

hat into the river washed his face and hands. He was bound south.

Penny Press, Saturday, August 15, 1885

DEEP RIVER

The old "leather man" passed through this village August 13th, bound South as usual. It is said that he is doing penance for some real or imaginary sin committed in his youthful days, but we do not interpret the scripture to mean that to be dirty will atone for sin. It

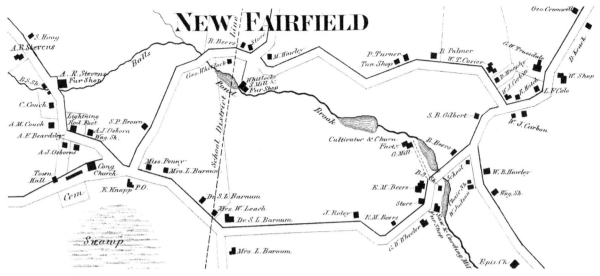

The Old Leather Man had a cave/rock shelter near Richard Hatch's residence in New Fairfield, Connecticut. F. W. Beers, Ellis, and Soule, Atlas of New York and Vicinity, 1867.

seems a pity that any persons religious belief should force them to wear a suit of leather in this hot weather, when old clothes can be had for two or three cents per pound, and brand new shirts for 25 cents at W. O. Post's.

Peekskill Blade, October 1885

The Leather Man

A TRAVELING HERMIT

THE LEATHER MAN AND
HIS ROMANTIC HISTORY
By L. G. Roake, Shrub Oak, N.Y.

There is no traveling man so well known among the farmers throughout Eastern New York and Western Connecticut as the "Leather Man." For 15 years or more he has been one of the chief objects of interest, as he has made his regular trips once a month, seldom varying an hour in his time of arriving at or starting from his customary stopping places. He is about 5 feet 8 inches in height and may weigh about 165 pounds. His complexion is very dark, either natural or from exposure, and he wears his beard trimmed rather short. His rude clothing is made entirely of leather, from the crown of his head to the soles of his feet. This strange wearing apparel is manufactured by himself, from small scraps of leather given him by the kindhearted farmers upon whom he makes his monthly calls. He never wears undergarments of any kind. Under his left

arm he carriers a large leather bag containing cigar stumps which he picks up along the highway, these are exchanged for sewing thread at a tobacco store in Connecticut. In his right hand he carries a heavy cane and he usually travels with his eyes resting upon the ground in quest of the coveted cigar stump. He is not looked upon as a tramp or beggar by the country folk, for he alone is exempt from prosecution in the recent law passed by the legislature against tramps.

For about fifteen years he has eaten breakfast once a month, between 9 and 10 A.M., with Mr. A. E. Ireland of Shrub Oak, Westchester County, N.Y. This is one of the very few places where the old fellow stops and here he exchanges no words. He asks for nothing, but eats what is given him without complaint or thanksgiving. He will eat no meat on Fridays and during the Lenten season he always kneels while partaking of his frugal meals. So regular are his habits that it is often said that he is the only sure thing that farmers can depend upon in this age of uncertainty.

In no weather will he take refuge in human habitation, but will spend the coldest nights in his rude caves along his route. His principle cave, or headquarters, in this Sawmill Valley woods, is about two miles south of Shrub Oak, near the New York City and Northern railroad. Here he spends one or two days every month in mending and oiling his unique clothing and making other preparations for his next tour through the Nutmeg State. In this lonely cave may be found a tin pail, an iron frying-pan, a small ax and a few shoemaker's tools, which he uses for tailoring, a bed of dry leaves held in place by several pieces of chestnut rail is the only unnecessary article of furniture in the dismal abode. At the foot of the hill the brook goes roaring and spattering over its rocky bed, and the ruins of the old sawmill, which has long since been deserted, stands like a faithful sentry guarding the crooked path that leads to the secluded domiciles.

His course is as fixed as that of the sun. Careful observation has established it as the same every month. He leaves Shrub Oak at 10 o'clock A.M., and proceeds to Jefferson Valley, thence via Somers Center to Brewster's, entering Connecticut near Ball's Pond and pursued a northeast direction through New Fairfield, Roxbury, Woodbury and Thomaston to his cave in Harwinton. Thence he goes through this town southeasterly through Berlin, Meriden and Middletown and follows the Connecticut River down to Old Saybrook. He then strikes west through Killingworth, Madison and Guilford. From here he goes around New Haven to Woodbridge, Orange, Stratford, North Bridgeport, Norwalk, into New Canaan. Turning northwest into Wilton, he takes a westerly course into New York State near the Portsmouth and Ridgefield Railroad. In New York he touches Purdy's Station, Mount Kisco, Croton Falls, Katonah, Croton Dam, Turkey mountain and Yorktown station, arriving at his sawmill valley cave at about sundown on the thirtieth day. Recently a photographer was able to get an instantaneous picture of him in full uniform as he was crossing Shrub Oak Plains and today the photograph may be found in almost every farmhouse from Peekskill to Hartford.

There has almost a superstition grown up around this quaint and mysterious individual. School children will seek refuge within the schoolhouse and view the "Leather Man" with fear and astonishment when he passes through a quiet country village. During these many years of his pilgrimage no one has been able to get any information from him as to whom he is or from whence he came, although he is often heard talking to himself in French as he slowly plods along his weary way. Every town has its legend and romances about the mysterious character, many of which have already been published, but the following points, which have been gathered after several years of painstaking investigation, are undoubtedly correct or nearly so:

He was born on the rural outskirts of the great city of Paris about 52 years ago. His parents though poor sent him to school during his early boyhood days and when he arrived at the age of 18 he entered a college in Paris. While there he met a beautiful French girl, an only daughter of a wealthy leather merchant, and a passionate love sprang up between them. When he left college at the age of 21, he told the leather merchant of his love for his daughter and asked for her hand in marriage. The father objected to the marriage on account of his being poor and unable to provide as grand a home for his daughter as she had always been accustomed to, but told him that he would take him into business as a partner and if he proved to be a successful business man at the end of five years, he might have his daughter and the business also. Delighted at this golden opportunity, he put forth all his energies and the business was prospering nobly under his management, when, at the end of the third year he invested in an immense stock of leather without consulting the senior members of the firm. Alas the panic came. Prices fell and the result was that this long-established business house was swept into bankruptcy. The old gentleman, seeing that he had been ruined, ordered the unfortunate young spectator from his house forever. The excitement attending this great financial crisis, together with the fact that the object of his affection was lost, perhaps never to be regained, drove the poor young man insane and he was placed in an asylum, where he spent several years, but was finally pronounced cured and released. Of course he went to Paris to find the young lady whom he loved so dearly. He was told that she had died with a broken heart. Her parents and his had also died and he realized the fact that he was left alone in the world without relatives, friends or money. He at once fled to America, where he has since been wandering from place to place, refusing to associate with any of his fellow beings, and waiting patiently for the time to come when his soul shall seek a kindlier country. He is a devout Catholic and always carries a little French prayer book next to his heart under his rude leather coat and around his neck hangs a small crucifix.

Just after a severe blizzard in February, he was passing a grocery store in the northern part of Westchester County. The storekeeper beckoned for him to come in. Contrary to his usual shyness he entered the store and took a seat that was offered him near the stove. His face bore marks of having been badly frozen. After eating some crackers and cheese, he was asked several questions but would make no reply. Finally, the storekeeper said, "I am so old (writing his age upon a piece of paper and handing him the pencil): how old are you?" The leather man took the pencil and slowly wrote 15342. What he really meant by these five rude figures is now a great puzzle to the people of that section. After refusing a paper of tobacco offered him by the storekeeper, he again started on his tramp with as firm and elastic a gait as he had when he traveled over the same road so many years ago.

On the 28th of April he was met on the street near Jefferson Valley by Mr. Augustus B. Field and asked several questions in French, to which he made no answer, but crossed to the opposite side of the street and moved silently forward as if wishing to avoid the intruder. Mr. Field turned and walked with him a short distance and continued to quiz his leather-ship, whereupon he raised his heavy cane in a threatening manner and said in French, "What do you want." Mr. Field concluded

The Old Leather Man crossing Shrub Oak Plains, New York, about 1885; photographer unknown. Leroy W. Foote collection.

that further interview was unnecessary and left the old fellow in great haste.

In his little prayer book, wrapped in silk paper, he carries a small portrait of the beautiful young lady above mentioned and he is frequently seen sitting by the road side gazing at this picture while the big tears trickle down his furrowed cheeks. The old fellow has no enemies but a host of friends in every town and it is considered in the light of heterodoxy for anyone to say aught against him.

[L. G. Roake,[14] Shrub Oak, N.Y.]

New York Times, Sunday, October 4, 1885

The Hermit of Saw Mill River

HOW A YOUNG FRENCHMAN

LOST A BRIDE AND A FORTUNE

In the upper part of Westchester County there lives a hermit, who is known in the vicinity as the "Leather Man." He is probably 50 years of age, and as far as can be learned, he was born and educated—for he is an educated man—in Paris, France. In early life he fell in love with the pretty daughter of a wealthy leather merchant in France, who frowned upon an alliance, as the prospective son-in-law was poor. He, however, took him into his business house, with the understanding that if at the end of two years he showed any business capac-

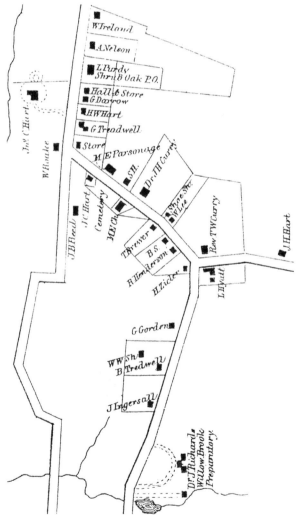

Shrub Oak, New York. F. W. Beers, Ellis, and Soule, Atlas of New York and Vicinity, 1867.

14. Lanning G. Roake, who died in Shrub Oak, New York, in 1930.

Old sawmill located on Mill Street near Stony Street in Shrub Oak, New York; postcard, early 1900s. A path near the ruins of the deserted sawmill leads to the Old Leather Man's cave/rock shelter in the Sawmill River valley woods. Leroy W. Foote collection.

ity the wedding might take place. With such a prize in prospect, the young man strained every nerve to achieve success. Presently, seeing what he considered a rare opportunity to invest in an immense stock of leather, he did so, but just then prices fell and the firm was bankrupted. The merchant then ordered the young man out of his sight forever. As a result, the daughter, so romance runs, pined for her lover for a short time and then sickened and died of a broken heart. Almost distracted, the dismissed suitor came to this country and plunged into the solitude of the upper part of Westchester County, and has wandered about aimlessly for many years, having his home in an old cave in the Sawmill River valley woods near Stony Street, two miles south of Shrub Oak. He makes his own clothing out of pieces of leather, which he sews together with stout twine. When thus attired he presents a very ludicrous appearance, but all who know him and his sad history pity him. He is very eccentric and will converse with nobody. Sometimes he extends his travels as far as New Haven. Although he has frequent offers of employment he will accept nothing from any one except provisions and leather. He is a devout Catholic, and observes the tenets of the church as far as he is able. He has a prayer book printed in French language, which he is often seen reading in the vicinity of his cave and while walking along the lonesome highways.

Deep River New Era, Friday, December 11, 1885

A Beautiful Gilt-Edge Panel, 5 x 8 Size,
Three Styles, of the Old Leather Man
Send post paid for 25 cents. Send to A. J. DAVISON,[15]
Box 530, Hartford, CT., or Deep River, Ct.

Another advertisement featured the woodcut, circa 1885 by an unknown artist. Advertisements using the woodcut ran off and on from 1885 to 1889 in local papers.

15. Albert J. Davison.

Davison's pictures of the "leather man" are selling fast.

Hartford Globe, December 1885

The Old Leather Man

HE DONS A WOOLEN SHIRT,—SOME NEW
FACTS ABOUT THE CURIOUS OLD MAN

Detail of the circa 1885 woodcut.

Some time ago the Globe gave a long history of this peculiar old character generally known in the state as the "Old Leather Man." Since then he has come into considerable notoriety and Mr. Hotchkiss of Forestville, one of the very few men who has the confidence of this strange being, writes us as follows:

"The Leather Man passed through Forestville Tuesday, the 22d, on his way south. The writer has succeeded in getting woolen garments on to him this winter. He seems much pleased with them and says he is very grateful to me for the interest taken in him. People that have noticed him for years say he has never been known to wear anything but leather. He talks very little English, but speaks (fluently) French and German. I have paid him a good deal of attention for the past four years and during that time he has never missed passing here once in 34 days. He will be due here again January 25th, 1886.

"I have visited him many times at his cave, which is about two miles south of this place. He never smiles and talks as one reads. He talks very reluctantly upon his life in the past, skillfully evading any points which would enable us to gain worthy information. *The more one knows concerning him, the more enigmatical he appears. I have arrived at this conclusion, that no mortal will ever know the real 'story of the Leather Man.'*[16]

"At one time he says he was born in Lyons, France; at another time in some other place. Then he talks disconnectedly about New Orleans. You ask him any questions which if answered would throw light upon the past and he answers: 'I don't know, I don't know.' So his curious existence is the shadow of mystery."

16. Emphasis Mr. Hotchkiss's, the author of the letter within the article.

Morning Journal and Courier, Sunday, January 10, 1886
NORTH HAVEN

The "old leather man" went through here last Friday and several who saw him remarked he looked very cold.[1]

Waterbury Daily American, Friday, January 22, 1886
FORESTVILLE

Is the "Leather Man" Dead?
The old leather man, who was due here the 25th, has not yet arrived, and it is feared that he has been frozen to death during the late severe norther while in New York state. Letters of inquiry are being sent to his stopping places to ascertain what has become of him.

Waterbury Daily American, Friday, January 29, 1886
FORESTVILLE

Frozen, but Not Dead
The old Leather Man passed through here the 27th, two days behind time, and his face bore the marks of having been frozen considerably.

Waterbury Daily American, Saturday, January 30, 1886
FORESTVILLE

He Still Lives and Talks
The Old Leather Man who passed through Forestville two days behind time said in answer to inquiry where he had been, "Shoes! Shoes! Shoes!" and holding up

1. Middletown's *Penny Press* newspaper noted on January 13, 1886, that "Monday night, the thermometer marked 26 below, Tuesday night only 24 [below zero]."

his foot showed a new pair which he had been making. The soles were of spruce wood about three fourths of an inch thick tapped with leather, the upper being fastened to the soles with bright No. 15 wire staples about half an inch in length, showing like a stitch. His face and neck were red as if frost bitten and pealing nearly all over the surface exposed. He was inclined to be more talkative than usual, but was disturbed by the school children that had been let out early to see him. He opened his coat to show that he had on a woolen shirt in response to questions and received a good supply of flannel shirts and stockings. He seemed to understand what was said to him and ate heartily of food, which was given him. He is not the man to avoid Forestville for fear his friends will photograph him.

Hartford Daily Courant, Saturday, January 30, 1886
NEWS OF THE STATE

A False Alarm About the "Leather Man"
The old "Leather Man" was first an interesting figure and then a great nuisance in the state papers. Of late he has been about as welcome as a request to print "Beautiful Snow." A Waterbury dispatch of Thursday said: "The old 'Leather Man,' who for thirty years has been the subject of so much mystery and speculation in eastern New York and western Connecticut, it is now believed has succumbed to the severe weather of the past month. It is known that he never sought shelter in human habitation in the severest weather, and never was known to converse with anyone further than to grunt out one or two French words when taken by surprise. He had huts and caves all along his route, from western New York through Connecticut, where he stopped regularly, and at one place in Forestville, where he has not failed to dine regularly once in thirty days for ten years, he has now been several days due. He was last seen in Woodbury, and it was thought that he must have perished in some of the neighboring mountains." Louis Kilby of Kensington wrote THE COURANT on Fri-

The Honorable Isaac W. Beach.

day that the "Leather Man" was all right. He saw him that day in Berlin.

Bristol Weekly Press, Thursday, February 4, 1886
FORESTVILLE

The "Old Leather Man" is not dead nor yet sleeping. He was only a day or two behind this month and his delay was caused by stopping to repair his footgear. He is the recipient of many presents of money, clothing and tobacco, every time he passes through this village and he rarely fails to stop at the residence of Hon. I. W. Beach, where he is always welcomed and fed.

Hartford Daily Courant, Thursday, February 4, 1886
NEWS OF THE STATE

A Practical View of the Case

If it had proven true that the "leather man" had frozen to death, it would have paid the newspapers of western Connecticut to have started another out.

Norwalk Gazette

Deep River New Era, Friday, February 5, 1886
ESSEX

The "old leather man," who it was feared had perished at one of his stopping places during the recent cold snap, passed through the town on Tuesday last. He stopped as usual at Aunt Azubah Starkey's[2] and got his lunch.

Port Chester Journal, Thursday, April 1, 1886

Connecticut's "Leather Man"

CAREER OF A WANDERING
TRAMP IN THE NUTMEG STATE

Almost everybody in Connecticut knows the "Leather Man." He is a queer old chap. Everything about him is leather. His hat, coat, breeches and traveling sack are made of coarse tanned stuff. It is seldom that this very eccentric individual speaks a word. Year in and year out he tramps about the State obtaining his food from the kindhearted people along the route. Always visiting the same house, knocking at the kitchen door and pointing to his mouth his wants are supplied. Whenever the mute appeal for victuals is refused the offending housewife is placed on his mental blacklist and her house is never visited a second time. A great deal of speculation has been indulged in by observers, who wonder what this man's story is. Why should he follow the same pathway around the same state as he has done for nearly half a century, with his face covered with a grizzled beard, his head cast down in his solemn tramp, tramp, tramp? Wiseacres in hamlets frequented by the "leather-man" are apt to say, "I know his history." Then they spin a long yarn of how, when a young man, this semi-respectable tramp loved a maiden fair. She would not have the aspiring shoemaker apprentice. His scorned affections sunk into melancholy. Unable to betake himself from the fascination of the world entirely, this stricken being resolved to encase his body in sole leather and become a pilgrim. So he began on the threshold of a promising career and so he promises to end, as a tramp.

A month ago he was reported frozen to death. The report was unfounded. He plods along as usual, friend-

2. "Aunt" Azubah (Congdon) Starkey (1802–1891), widow of Austin Starkey, lived in Essex on the Middlesex Turnpike (now Route 154). Her home still stands today.

Residence of "Aunt" Azubah (Congdon) Starkey and her stepson William "Billie" Starkey, Essex, Connecticut. Courtesy of the Don Malcarne collection.

less and uncared for, still offering food for gossiping tongues of ever-wondering citizens in the peaceful towns on the line of his march.

New Haven Daily Palladium, Wednesday, June 23, 1886

NORTH HAVEN

The Leatherman passed westward Tuesday, Hour and ½ later than usual time.

Meriden Journal, Thursday, August 19, 1886

That Leather Man

HE ASTONISHED THE NATIVES

BY DINING AT WOODBURY HOTEL

The "Leather Man" passed through Woodbury on his regular trip Tuesday, and for the first time in the history of that town, although the thing has been tried many, many times before, was induced to go into a house and eat a meal. It was about 10:30 a.m. when he came toiling along the road in front of the Parker house, itself one of the most hospitable looking country hotels in the state. When he came along there last, a woman from the house tried to coax him in, but in vain. Tuesday the same women tried it again, beckoned and told him to come and get a bowl of coffee. Without more ado than as if he were accustomed to it, the walking mystery passed up the carriage drive and into the kitchen. He deposited his rather huge and ungainly grip-sack of rough leather, containing his axe and other utensils, by his side as he sat down by the table to a huge plate of substantial food. Throwing back his leather coat, which is like a long officer's cape, and sleeveless, he revealed a scanty, rudely mended, dark-colored woolen shirt, which was open at the throat, showing a broad expanse of chest not unlike that of an ox, both for muscle and color. A string was about his neck, but no talisman was

Broadway, looking west, North Haven, Connecticut, postcard early 1900's.

apparent. His shoes were very pointed—so only a year or two out of date—and the soles of them were two or three inches thick. His trousers were of the present wide-flowing pattern, and were made of pieces from one or two feet square, spiked together as if it were with huge throngs. His cap was "to match."

He soon had devoured all the bread and ham. He disdained the beefsteak but grunted an affirmative when two more mammoth bowls of coffee were offered him. The interested spectators kept well in the background for fear of making him shy another time. One, however, when he neglected to answer the cook, asked him in French if he would have some butter. Then for the first time he looked up and fixed his steel gray eyes intently on the speaker, though he only answered with an unintelligible guttural. Perhaps "butter" or "burre" is not in his vocabulary: "oleomargarine" certainly cannot be. He ate enough for three hearty men, then refused everything else and would not put any in his haversack. With another guttural he took his departure. A boarder touched his hat and said "Good day, sir," to which the pilgrim replied with a very pleasant look and nod of his head as he went on his way to his new cave. He had lately abandoned his old cave in that town for one nearer by, probably because he found that the former was too often visited. His hair fell in scant ringlets to his shoulders. His beard was black and fairly well trimmed,

not heavy enough to cover the whole of a very weather-beaten face.

Morning Journal and Courier, Connecticut, Friday, August 20, 1886

That Leather Man
The leather man was in Woodbury on his regular trip Tuesday, and for the first time was induced to go into a house and eat a meal. He was seen in Lanesville near the Lovers' Leap on Sunday last.

Woodbury Reporter, Thursday, August 19, 1886

Advertisement that appeared in the Woodbury Reporter.

The Parker House, about 1885. Now the home of "The Elemental Garden," 359 Main Street, South Woodbury, Connecticut. Courtesy of the Robert B. Cowles collection.

New York Times, Sunday, August 22, 1886

A Connecticut Mystery

THE OLD LEATHER MAN STILL ON THE TRAMP

HE APPEARS ONCE IN 34
DAYS, BUT NEVER SPEAKS
A Strange Being in Strange Garb

Woodbury, Conn., Aug. 21. This historic little town has experienced an excitement this week hardly less powerful, if more wholesome, than that of last week when Robert Drakeley shot his bride through the heart. The Leather Man stopped at a human residence and ate; and, what was stranger still, that human residence was a hotel. For years this traveling mystery has trudged through this town, as he has through so many others of no greater population, from southeastern New-York to the Connecticut River, speaking to no one and stopping only at a remote cave on the mountain side. Many and many a time have the good people along this route tried to coax him in, in fair weather or in foul, to partake of some nourishment, but all in vain. From earliest recollections he has remained in himself a mystery as profound as any for which Connecticut is noted. His ordinary habits are already well known to the readers of THE TIMES.

With almost no variation he makes his appearance at each place along his route once in 34 days. The last time he passed through here an attempt was made by a woman at the Parker House, itself a very comfortable country hostelry, to get him to stop. This time the woman was on the lookout for him. At precisely the same hour he came along the same path. Running out, the woman beckoned and shouted: "Come here and get a bowl of coffee." At once the quaint fellow, who is said to understand no English, turned and followed her to the kitchen where a huge platter of meat, potatoes and bread was put before him. For the first time the people had a chance to get a fair study of him. Depositing on the floor his huge gripsack of rough leather, in which he carried his axe and other tools, he threw back his variegated leather tunic and revealed beneath a particolored woolen shirt, mended and re-mended. This was open enough at the neck to show a breast, which had about the same color and consistency as than of an ox. His trousers were of the latest London fashion, wide flowing to bagginess and were composed of two-foot patches of leather joined by rude leathern thongs. His shoes were shaped something like a Chinaman's with soles at least three inches thick. On his head he wore a cap made to match his grotesque uniform. The whole apparel looked to be about 200 years old. The man himself probably is not over 45. He measures about 5 feet 7, erect figure and firm, solid flesh. His hair straggles out from under his cap in scanty ringlets to his shoulders, his beard is black, with hardly a trace of gray and decently trimmed.

While these observations were being made by *The Times* correspondent the man had fairly licked his platter clean, barring the beefsteak, of which he was wary—evidence, perhaps, that he once lived in a boarding house. In addition he had drank three large bowls of coffee. The cook asked him if he would have butter on his bread. To this as to all else he only answered with a deep guttural. The newspaperman then put the question to him in French, his supposed native language. Thereupon the mystery leaned over the table and with his steel blue eyes, as some civilized men do when they suspect an interview, then settled back with another unintelligible grunt. He may have been afraid of oleomargarine. When fully satisfied, he refused to put anything in his haversack, grasped his heavy cane and started out with a very pleasant nod and grunt to the newspaperman, to make his way to the cave on the mountain.

The news spread like wildfire through the street and

a constant string of visitors came to the house to see if anything new had been learned about the perennial, obstinate, yet half-revered, mystery about which these people have heard since they were children. And herein lies the mystery, the solution of which must be forever locked up within the leathern breast. How is it, if the old people remember him as an old man when they were young, that he is so young looking now? Must it not be that he is a successor to the original leather man? If so, has he ever penetrated his predecessor's secret or does he know ought of his final disposition? How is it that this leathern mantel has fallen to him since the other man was just as solitary and self-contained? What could have been any one's object in becoming such a dumb, tramping successor? The tramp law of the state, it should be said, makes an exception of this man and that person would be in danger of the tar barrel and feather bed who should even breathe a suspicion that the leather man could have been guilty of any one of Connecticut's mysterious crimes. The reporter peered into the carpetbag in vain for the head and limbs of the Wallingford murder man.

So the old man will keep on tramping until some day he is missed, when a searching party will as surely be made up for him as would be for the best citizen and he will be found dead in the woods or his skeleton may add still another mystery to the long list. He need only keep out of the way of Connecticut murder detectives and that need not be very difficult.

New Milford Gazette, Friday, August 27, 1886
ROXBURY

At last the "Old Leather man" is photographed and at a time when he least expected it. One day recently, while he was being entertained at his usual lunching place in the Center, a camera was placed in a doorway that he always passes, and when he again started on his tramp, all was in readiness. As he reached the important door he was met, seemingly by accident, and a newspaper offered him. As he stopped to receive it an instantaneous view was taken. He heard some noise, and glancing up, saw the camera. He started in haste without asking, as most people under the circumstances do, when he could see the proof. But all who were in the plot are waiting anxiously to see the result.

Bristol Weekly Press, Thursday, January 6, 1887
FORESTVILLE

Some one sent the "Old Leather Man," in care of I. W. Beach, Esq., an almanac printed in French. Mr. Beach saw him Wednesday and gave him the book, which greatly pleased the old fellow, as he could readily read it.

He was two days behind, owing to stormy weather, but aside from having an unusually smoky appearance was all right.

Bristol Weekly Press, Thursday, April 28, 1887
FORESTVILLE

Thursday was the "Old Leather Man's" day. As he passed through the village he was followed by Nash and Troy, two persons of doubtful reputations, who are reported to have assaulted the old man as he was passing the house of Simon Young. Isaac Spencer visited the hut[3] Thursday, but failed to see its occupant and repeating his visit Sunday, found the hut in confusion and its contents scatted far and wide. Fears are entertained that the singular traveler will change his route and will be seen on our streets no more.

Waterbury Daily American, Friday, April 29, 1887
FORESTVILLE

Was the Old Leather Man Assaulted?
The community is thoroughly aroused by the report that the old Leather Man was ill-treated and abused by Daniel Nash and Patsey Troy on his trip through here April 21 after passing Kinney's hill toward his hut, which is a few miles below in the woods near Isaac Spencer's. It is only from a lack of positive proof of the misconduct toward the old man that the offenders have not been made to realize the extent of the indignation felt by paying the penalty of the law. It is stated that Nash and Troy were in liquor and followed the Leather man, attempting to make him receive and eat things by using force. Troy says that the report is untrue, and claims that no force or violence was used against the old man; but, on the contrary, they gave him something to

3. On the side of Red Stone Hill in Plainville, Connecticut.

drink from the bottle of liquor in the possession of Nash, and 20 cents was taken for the drink because the old man insisted on paying for it. Troy further says that they tried to buy bread for him at Mr. Young's and did so at John Dignan's, carrying the bread to the old man's hut but, when they arrived before him, that he sat down and began to read a paper a little way from the hut when he saw them there. He declares they were sober and did not disturb the object of their curiosity, but nevertheless citizens believe from what has been said by people who live on that road, and saw Troy and Nash, that they went through the old man. Mr. Spencer, who usually carries him a supper to the hut, says he found everything in confusion within and no one there, and he knows he did not stop in his hut as usual that night. Also a portion of the shelter was burned. This is suggested by Nash's admission that they built up a big fire there. The circumstances seem to clearly indicate that something unusual occurred causing the old man to abandon his rude lodging, but to what extent he was interfered with can best be determined by his next visit. It is believed that he will avoid Forestville altogether and not return to his old camp. If this should be so it would be conclusive evidence that he was maltreated by some one, and it would be useless for those accused to enter a denial. Nash left town a day or two after the affair and is reported to be in Winsted. The matter will be investigated thoroughly, and it is hoped for the reputation of this locality that there may be more truth in Troy's statement than people are inclined at present to believe. He says he is willing to go before a justice and challenge any one to implicate them in any abuse whatever of the old man. Every man, woman and child is in sympathy with the Leather Man, and ill fares the pusillanimous rascal who dares to harm him and is proven guilty.

Waterbury Daily American, Thursday, May 5, 1887
FORESTVILLE

What They Say About the Alleged Assault on the Leather Man

A careful investigation of the circumstances connected with the alleged treatment of the Old Leather man by Daniel Nash and Patsey Troy recently tends to confirm the report that he was wrongfully used and interfered with. The full extent of the attack is not known, as some

three hours passed after his passing from sight by the last house on the road before Troy and Nash returned (the inhabitants say) under the influence of liquor. The children along the road agree in their statements that these men followed the old man who hastened and looked behind frequently and at one place he would not stop to drink a bowl of tea, but, seeing his pursuers coming, took the food offered him and hurried on, and when they were about to overtake him he turned out to one side of the road and sat down. Troy and Nash approached and the three remained there some 10 minutes. During this time, some boys say, the old man was crying and his tormentors were trying to make him take off his hat and cross himself, which he refused to do. They offered him a bottle of liquor, but he would not receive it till they had first tasted it. Then the old man took it and apparently drank to accommodate them, but as though he did not care for it. This is the liquor, which Troy said the old man insisted on paying for and for which they took 20 cents to accommodate him. This proceeding was broken up by the old man who slung his leather bag over his shoulder and started off, as if he was mad. At the house of Thomas Gerraty they bought five cents worth of bread and proceeded to the hut where Troy admits they arrived first, but what transpired after leaving the main road cannot be positively stated. The hut was afterward found to contain a quantity of dead limbs not as the old man usually left them. The last fire had burned over a portion of the surface not used as the fire place, and this was not cleaned out as usual, ready for the next visit. Mr. Young's children informed I. W. Beach of the matter, going up to Forestville more than a mile for the purpose, but Mr. Beach did not attach enough importance to the report to go to see about it, yet he says the children told him the fellows were plaguing the old man and he was crying. These are the facts so far as it is possible to gain information, and they are presented with no reference to any one further than the truth demands in justice to this strange and harmless wanderer who should be protected by all means against unkind treatment.

Bristol Weekly Press, Thursday, May 26, 1887
FORESTVILLE

The "old leather man" passed through this village about 6 o'clock Tuesday evening. He was one day ahead of time and it would not have been safe for any one to have molested him. Great indignation is felt that his assailants of last month have been allowed to go Scot-free. They should have been prosecuted.

New Haven Evening Register, Friday, June 3, 1887
FROM THE BIG VILLAGE

Looking For the Leather Man

New York, June 3.—An old Frenchmen was unloaded at the barge office at the battery the other day who made inquiries almost as soon as he got ashore for Jules Bourglay, who, he said, had been living the life of a recluse in this country for more than thirty years. His story, as told at a French boarding house down town, fits strangely into that of a man many Connecticut people know something about. It was to the effect that Bourglay when a young man was connected with a large mercantile establishment in an interior city of France and that he had advanced in business there, showing such remarkable aptitude and capabilities that he had finally assumed the charge of his employer's extensive interest, the latter retiring from active labor. About this time Bourglay became engaged to the young, beautiful and accomplished daughter of his employer and the preparations for the wedding were already advanced when a financial crash came that swept his employer's business out of sight in an instant almost and in some way, the aged Frenchman could not tell how, separated Bourglay and his promised bride.

There were many discrepancies in the tale of the narrator, but the above is the substance of his story up to the time of the crash.

How Bourglay came to come to America and why, he could not tell. He knew that he did come here, however, and had been wandering about the country ever since in a sort of demented state. Neither did he know what had become of the fiancée.

Now comes the queer part of the old man's story. He says that Bourglay was born in Paris and was the son of a butcher. He left his home at an early age, some time after his disappearance from France; Bourglay pere drew the capital prize in a Spanish lottery, amounting to some $50,000, and soon after died. This money has been a public charge ever since. The old Frenchman claims to have been sent over here to find Bourglay and to see that the fortune is placed in his possession. He

(the Frenchman) is promised a reward of $10,000 if he can find Bourglay.

Not much confidence is put in the man's story by well informed French people. They say that the authorities of their country do not send people out looking after lost money in that way. The story of "the old leather man," who for years has constituted a Connecticut mystery, was, however, rehearsed to him and it is possible that the old fellow may come tramping out that way. His story is much like that related of the leather man and I believe the latter's name is Jules Bourglay.

New York World, Sunday, June 19, 1887

Will the Leather Man Appear
A RECLUSE FOR WHOM $50,000 AND AN OLD FLAME ARE SAID TO BE WAITING.

(SPECIAL TO THE WORLD)

Bridgeport, June 19. Great interest has suddenly been aroused in the "Leather Man," a recluse whose story *The World* published, with illustration, about two years ago. Until lately he has had regular intervals of appearing in certain localities. He dressed in leather and was known to have a hut in the hills between Newtown and Meriden. Recently the hut was destroyed and it was discovered by some hunters that it had been sacked and everything about it mutilated or scattered around, evidently by a marauding party. It is feared that the leather man met with foul play, as he has not been seen since.

The great interest in him has been intensified by the appearance in town of Jules Martins, an aged Frenchman, who has just arrived from France. He is looking for Jules Bourglay. The old Frenchman is promised $10,000 reward if he can find Jules Bourglay. As the name of the leather man is known to be Bourglay and his time for appearing at sundown June 20, much curiosity is manifested in the result of the meeting of Martins and Bourglay.

Martins' story is that Bourglay when a young man was connected with a large mercantile establishment in an interior city of France and that he advanced rapidly in the business there, showing such remarkable aptitude and capabilities that he finally assumed the charge of his employer's extensive interest, the latter retiring from active labor. About this time Bourglay became engaged to the young, beautiful and accomplished daughter of his employer and the preparations for the wedding were already well advanced when a financial crash came that swept away his employer's capital and separated Bourglay and his loved one.

Martins heard that Bourglay came to America and had been wandering about ever since in a demented state. He says that Bourglay's father died leaving $50,000, which has been a public charge ever since. Jules Martins says he has been sent over here to find Jules Bourglay and he believes that the leather man is the man he is seeking. The odd part of Martins' story is that the young lady, whom Bourglay loved also, became demented. She still lives in France and talks of nothing but of Bourglay. Jules Martins hopes that if he can meet the leather man and show him the photograph of the girl, Bourglay's reason may be restored and that he may return to France and take possession of his fortune and call back his loved one to reason and happiness.

New York World, Monday, June 20, 1887

The New Haven Register of June 3 gives similar accounts of the leather man, of which we give a few extracts:

He, the old Frenchman, says that Bourglay was born in Paris and was the son of a butcher. He left his home at an early age. Sometime after his disappearance from France, Bourglay pere drew the capital prize in a Spanish lottery, amounting to some $50,000, and soon after died. This money has been a public charge ever since. Not much confidence is put in the man's story by well-informed French people. They say that the authorities of their country do not send people out looking after lost money in that way. The story of "the old leather man," who for years has constituted a Connecticut mystery, was, however, rehearsed to him and it is possible that the old fellow may come tramping out that way. His story is much like that related of the leather man and I believe the latter's name is Jules Bourglay.

C. L. Hotchkiss has letters in his possession from Mr. Rodgers of Branford, claiming that the leather man's name is I. Zak. However, it is possible that this mind-depraved individual, who has long been a curiosity to the village, may be the heir to a vast amount of wealth. It can be noticed in the above that he was expected in Bridgeport last Monday night, but we have not heard as yet whether Martins met the leather man as intended.

We received the following in answer to an inquiry:

Sir; The old Leather Man passed through here May 4th, was due last week, but has not been seen. Will let you know of his movements in this vicinity.
    Yours,
    John R. Comstock[4]
    Wilton, Conn., June 12, 1887

Deep River New Era, Friday, July 8, 1887
ESSEX

The old Leather man, of whom so much has been published in the different newspapers, lately passed through this village on his weary tramp southward last Wednesday, about noon. He as it's been his custom for the past thirty years, stopped at Aunt Azubah Starkey's and partook of his lunch. It is said by those who saw him, that he appeared in feeble health and his steps seemed tottering. No doubt but what the poor old man's pilgrimage is fast drawing to a close, and the probabilities are he may never tramp his old route again or at least but a few years longer, and it is hoped that the rumor of his falling heir to a fortune may prove true, and that his declining years may be passed in peace and luxury.

Shoreline Times, Friday, August 19, 1887
BRANFORD NEWS, FRIDAY

The Leather Man passed through this place Monday 3 days behind time. The warm weather and old age plays on the constitution of this wonderful prodigy.

Penny Press, Middletown, Connecticut, Wednesday, November 30, 1887
MIDDLEFIELD

The leather man passed the house of Mr. Sanford Coe sabbath morning last. This character makes monthly rounds through the north part of Middletown, and his route always is from the northwest to southeast.

---

4. John R. Comstock was the station master at the Wilton depot.

The Old Leather Man, photographed at the Bradley Chidsey House in Branford, Connecticut, by James F. Rodgers, 1887.

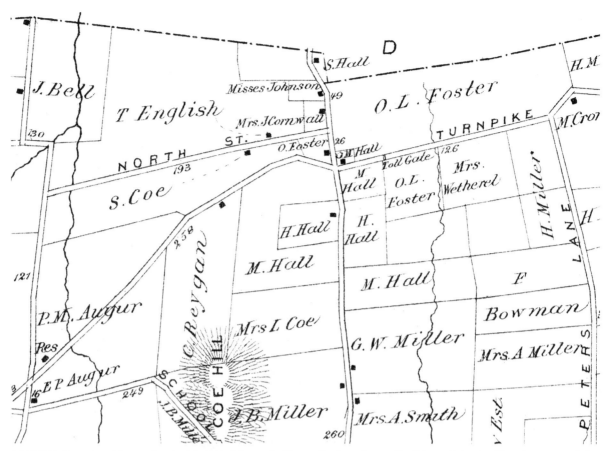

Middlefield, Connecticut. After spending the night in his shelter north of Preston Notch, on the east side of Mount Higby, the Old Leather Man traveled east on North Street, passing the home of Middlefield farmer Sanford Coe (upper left center, on map). He then turned right onto Higby Road and stopped at Amy Guy's house; Mrs. Guy lived adjacent to her father, Oliver Lyman Foster (upper right center). From there, the Old Leather Man headed east on the Middlesex Turnpike (now Route 66) into Middletown. Near the intersection of Boston Road, he stopped for food at the home of Susan Fisher, whose husband, John, and son, Hiram, operated Fisher's Gristmill. W. Beers, Atlas of Middlesex County, Connecticut, 1874.

Mr. Coe has known the leather man for 20 years, and always going the same route as that mentioned. Lately the wanderer has made calls at the house of Mrs. Amy Guy and been supplied with food. From Mrs. Guy's he goes on the turnpike, past Fisher's gristmill, and takes the right hand road passing through the woods near Mr. A. M. Colegrove's.

Penny Press, Monday, January 9, 1888

EAST BERLIN

The Old Leather Man passed through the town a week ago Sunday going south. He goes over Savage Hill, and

Fisher's Gristmill became the Old Mill—Wayside Furniture. The building stood until 2007, when it was taken down to allow for the widening of Route 66.

Fisher's Gristmill is the large building to the right of the bridge (this photograph was taken looking south); postcard, early 1900s.

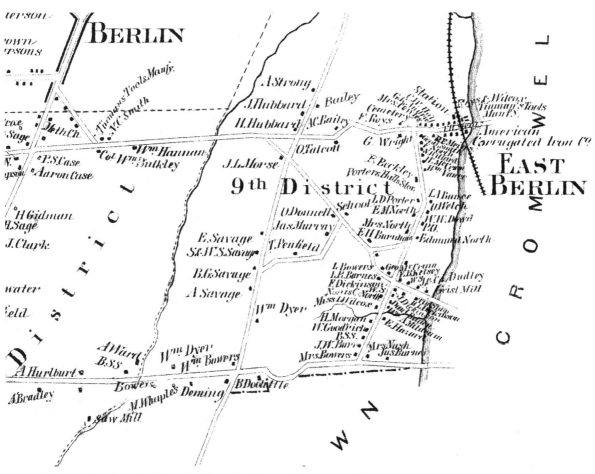

Savage Hill, East Berlin. Baker and Tilden, Atlas of Hartford County, Connecticut, 1869.

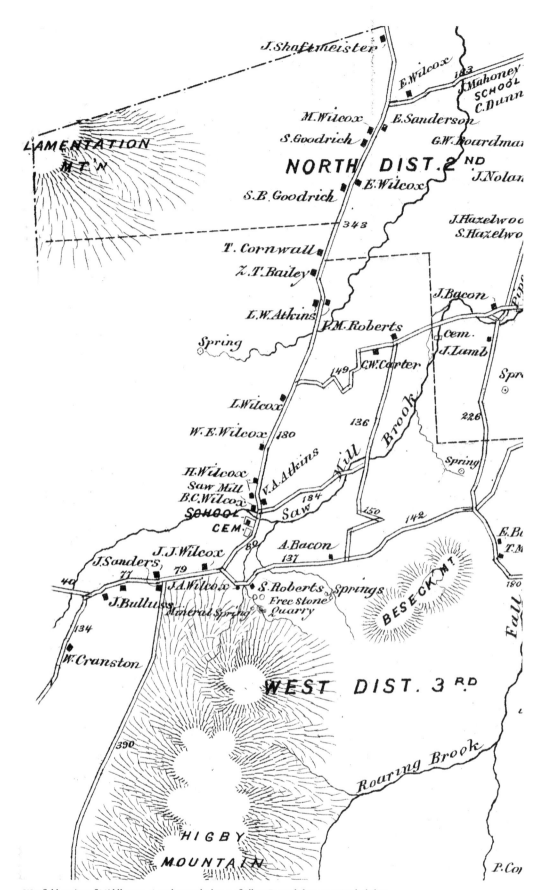

Westfield section of Middletown. A path near the home of Albert Bacon led to a cave/rock shelter on the east side of Mount Higby. F. W. Beers, Atlas of Middlesex County, Connecticut, 1874.

stops sometime at Ryan's[5] in Westfield for a bite. He stops, if invited to, before he reaches a certain point. After reaching that nothing will induce him to come back.

Near Albert Bacon's he has a cave in which he stops nights.

Morning News, Saturday, February 11, 1888

Woes of the Wanderer

THE LEATHER MAN OUTRAGED
BY HOODLUMS OF THE FOREST

HIS FROZEN APPEARANCE ACCOUNTED
FOR ATROCITIES WHICH MAY HAVE BEEN
INSPIRED BY LITCHFIELD COUNTY BRANDY

A shocking story of cruelties which unknown men perpetrated on that defenseless old wanderer, the "leather man," with the intention, perhaps, of being funny, comes from Terryville.

At a point where the towns of Plymouth, Bristol and Harwinton come together, and two miles from any house, is a lonely habitation, partly a hut and partly a cave. In it the old Frenchman sleeps when his monthly rounds brings him there, with a rude bed of pine boughs at the end of the cave which is covered with branches, and his fire of logs at the open end. Before he leaves the place on each journey he provides the fuel for the next visit. A spring of the purest water bubbles perennially near the place and another advantage of the location which shows the forethought of the old man is that it is the most sheltered place of that mountain region. His food, of course, he brings from elsewhere, for there is nothing obtainable there, and the only game, if he had the means of securing it, is the nimble squirrel and the fox. The cave is in a ledge of rocks, which has a history. In the revolutionary war there were many Tories in the towns about, and they were diligently persecuted by the patriotic Americans. Many a night the loyalists were obliged to flee from their homes and seek refuge in the forests; and the hole in the rocks, about 50 yards from the "leather man's cave," is yet known as the "Tory's Den." C.W. Cook, esq., owns the land and has for years been a protector of his uninvited tenant, but

recently Mr. Cook and family removed to Yalesville, and that fact probably explains the liberty that youths in question took with the demented loner last week.

STORY OF THE ATROCITIES

Lute Welton is a boy of 18 or 19, who spends his time, winter and summer, in hunting or fishing, and acts as guide to villagers who visit the "Tory Den" or the Frenchman's cave. He is a redheaded, freckled and bashful young fellow, with a vocabulary limited, so far as has yet been ascertained by strangers, to "yes" and "no." Last Saturday morning he took his dog and gun and went to the woods on a rabbit hunt. In the course of the day the boy arrived in sight of the leather man's stopping place and seeing the old fellow, approached him. He appeared to be partially frozen, and finding that young Welton was friendly showed him that the brush part of his place of shelter was recently burned. The backwoods youth understood the situation instinctively, and it was perhaps an expression of sympathy in the freckled face that led the usually suspicious Frenchman to further reveal his woes. His woodpile had also been burned. "I sleep," he explained. Then he led the boy to his little spring. The water, in a sheltered pool, was unfrozen except around the edges. Lute could see nothing wrong, but the old man took a tin cup out of the small sack, which is a part of his coat, and dipped up some water. Lute tasted of it. The liquid was bitterly salt.

PROBABLY THE WORK OF WOODSMEN

Poor old Bourglay, if that be his name, had lost on that cold night his shelter and firewood through the deviltry of some unknown parties, who probably thought that it was a joke, and as a result his hands and face were partially frozen.[6] That the deviltry had been previously planned is indicated by the provision of the salt, but it is possible that the outragers were charcoal-burners or woodchoppers who had been living on the woods and carried the salt on that account.

The leather man would not go to Lute's home as the boy begged him to, but took his immense bag and started onward, probably to find some other cave in the

5. Thomas Ryan, a farmer, lived on West Street.

6. About that time, the thermometers registered fifteen degrees below zero in the nearby town of Winsted, according to the Hartford Courant of February 1, 1888.

"Tory's Den," Burlington, Connecticut, located at the corners of the towns of Burlington, Plymouth, Bristol, and Harwinton, postcard, early 1900s. The man pictured is said to be Lute Welton. Another cave/rock shelter stands about 150 yards to the east. Courtesy of the Plymouth Historical Society.

same forest, for he has never been known to return to any place where he had been molested.

Penny Press, Monday, February 13, 1888

Badly Frozen

The Old Leather Man passed through Centerbrook Saturday. He presented a pitiable appearance, as both his ears and face had been terribly frozen. Still he was only a few days behind time.

Hartford Times, Tuesday, February 17, 1888
FORESTVILLE

The Old Leather Man

The old leather man crossed the railway in this village four days behind his scheduled time. He was a pitiful object. The cold weather, which he braved for so many years, laid its hands on the old fellow recently with telling effect. His face, neck and chest had been frozen badly.

His ears were swollen as large as a man's hand. The *New Haven News* explains his condition that woodsmen burned his hut at the corner formed by the towns of Plymouth, Bristol and Harwinton and took away his fire wood.

Penny Press, Monday, March 12, 1888

A Terrible Snow[7]
TRAINS BLOCKED ON ALL ROADS

THE HEAVIEST FALL OF SNOW AND
THE MOST SEVERE STORM FOR
YEARS—TRAFFIC AT A STANDSTILL

Early last evening snow began to fall and at daybreak this morning fully six inches of the beautiful [stuff] covered the ground. The wind blew with such velocity as to drift the snow in every direction, blocking the railroads and traffic is now at a stand still. One car, with four horses, started out a few minutes before seven this morning, on the street railroad, and with difficulty made the round trip. No more cars left the barn. The restaurants and hotels were crowded at noon with people who were unable to reach their homes. Telegraph, telephone and electric wires are down, and business on the street in general is suspended. Conductor Beck with the Valley road, says that he experienced no difficulty until he reached Higganum and from there he met great drifts until he reached the poor house, about three miles below this city, where the train came to a short stop. Two engines were dispatched from this city and brought the train out of its difficulty. The 11:35 train on the Air Line has not yet been heard from at the Union depot. The train that leaves Berlin on the Branch road shortly after eight o'clock was the only one that reached this city to-day on that road, and it is now blocked near the engine house in this city, where it arrived two and one-half hours behind time.

The first Valley train from Hartford and the Air Line from Willimantic arrived all right this morning, but the snow storm delayed all other trains. Holman's train from Saybrook was 45 minutes late at Higganum, and it got stuck in a snow drift about one mile south of this city. The engine got out of water, so it left the train in the snow, and came here to replenish. Having quenched the thirst of the iron horse, the engine returned to the

7. The Blizzard of 1888 began on Monday, March 11. Heavy snow, often accompanied by raging winds, continued for nearly four days. When it finally ended on March 14, New England and New York were thoroughly buried. In Connecticut, Middletown recorded *fifty inches* of snowfall. Clinton residents dug through fifteen-foot drifts to get out of their homes. The Old Leather Man, according to the newspapers, holed up in one of his cave/rock shelters in the eastern part of Southington for the duration of the storm.

train and brought it to this city. The train, which usually leaves this city at 10:12 for Saybrook, was delayed here until Holman's train arrived. The train from New Haven, which usually leaves here at 8:53 a.m. for Willimantic, was unable to leave to-day until 10:30 a.m.

The Valley train from Saybrook referred to above was at noon still stuck in a snow drift one mile below the city, and the 10:12 train south was side-tracked at Union depot, waiting for the up train.

The Air Line train, which left here at 10:30 a.m. for Boston, came to a stand still east of the Portland station, and had not reached the Portland station, and had not reached Cobalt at noon.

Meriden Daily Republican, Tuesday, March 13, 1888

The Big Storm
NOTHING LIKE IT EVER SEEN IN THIS CITY

SNOW BANKS UP TO THE
SECOND STORY WINDOWS.
Half a Dozen Locomotives Stalled Near the Corner.
Feeding Water to Them with Hose This Morning.
Men and Women Train-Bound and Hungry.
WOMEN FAINT TRYING TO GET HOME.

Girls Sleeping and Eating in the Factories.
Meriden Employers Looking Out for Their Hands.
Business at a Complete Stand Still.
THE STORY IN MERIDEN.
Scenes of the Great Storm.
Events of Mondays Graphically Described by "Republican" Reporters.

The storm, which began in a light squall Sunday night at about 5 o'clock, and which kept intermitting between snow, rain, wind and cloudy weather through the night, burst with all its fury about 5 o'clock Monday morning, and was evidently centered about Meriden. At this time the snow began to fall with most terrific force and the wind began to blow violently. By the time people were ready to go to their work in the shops there was a foot of snow on a level, where it could be measured, and the storm was increasing in force. Most of the shop employees who live in the suburbs managed to drive in all right, little imagining the terrible siege which was before them. School children in many cases, not knowing the exact conditions of the weather, started for the school house, but many of them turned back before reaching their destinations. Those who did reach the schools were very wisely soon sent home by the teachers.

Blizzard of 1888: three trains at Meriden Station. Courtesy of the Meriden Historical Society.

Blizzard of 1888: Meriden House. Courtesy of the Meriden Historical Society.

THE CONSOLIDATED ROAD

was taken completely by surprise, having hosed its snow plows a week before in anticipation of spring weather. The trouble began at Meriden, and the worst trouble was centered about here. The 7:21 down train was the first to experience difficulty. It became stalled just south of the depot, and for over a half hour worked to get started on its way.

At Cooper street another trouble was met, but the engine and trainmen struggled bravely and got into New Haven at about 10 o'clock in the forenoon. The 8:44 down and the 9:01 arrived in Meriden only a few minutes behind time, but their difficulty came between Meriden and New Haven and the 9:01 train pulled into New Haven yard at about 5 o'clock in the afternoon. The 11:06 down train pulled out of Hartford only 20 minutes behind time, but didn't arrive at its final resting place opposite Foster & Merriam's factory until about 2 p.m. Here the most violent exertions of four engines failed to budge the train further.

THE STREETS

were in awful condition. Superintendent Barker, of the Horse railroad, thinking with others that the storm must soon abate, ran out the big snow plow at an early hour and attempted to keep the track open. He gave it up before noon, for the snow would drift in faster than it could be plowed out. Drifts in many cases 12 or 15 feet in height formed in an incredibly short time, and numerous tips over resulted from attempts to pull teams

through. Several slight runaways were reported, but nothing extensive. On East Main street, opposite the Meriden bank building, was one of the highest drifts, and on West Main street, in front of the Meriden house, was another of great height, but there were others which would bear excellent comparison to those scattered in the more infrequently-traveled streets.

Penny Press, Tuesday, March 20, 1888

Views of the Storm

Moore, the photographer, took about 50 views of the city during and after the great storm. They are choice works of art, and can be seen and purchased at his studio, 158 Main street.

Penny Press, Saturday, March 17, 1888

EAST BERLIN

The Old Leather Man put in an appearance yesterday morning,[8] stopping for breakfast at W. M. Fowler's. He was headed east and looked as well as he usually does.

8. At this point most roads remained buried under two or three feet of snow, and trains were unable to reach Southington until the end of the day. Somehow, the Old Leather Man was able to dig out of his Southington cave and make his way to Berlin in time for breakfast at the home of William and Harriet Fowler.

Blizzard of 1888: Young Men's Christian Association—Moore's Photograph Studio—"Doc" McKee's Drugstore, Main Street, Middletown.
Courtesy of the Middlesex County Historical Society.

Hartford Courant, **Monday, March 19, 1888**

SOUTHINGTON

The Old Leather Man
The "Old Leather Man" remained in a cave in the eastern part of this town during the storm.

Penny Press, **Thursday, March 22, 1888**

CHESTER

The Leather man passed through here yesterday going south.

The schools were closed all last week owing to the snow being so deep as to prevent the scholars from attending.

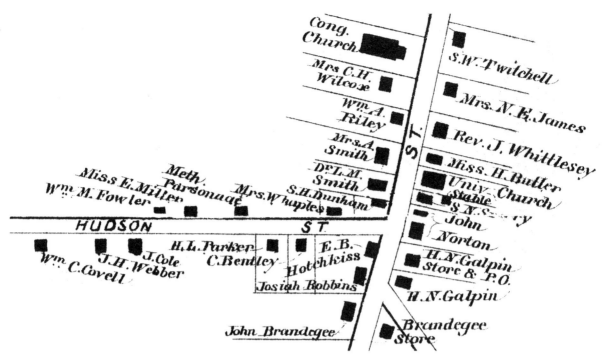

Berlin, Connecticut: William and Harriet Fowler home at left. Baker and Tilden, Atlas of Hartford County, Connecticut, 1869.

Bristol Weekly Press, Thursday, March 22, 1888

A beautiful oil painting of "The Old Leather Man at Home" is on exhibition at W. A. Terry's store. It was executed by artist Benham, of New Haven and represents a forest view in Branford with the Leather Man's rude hut near a little stream, with the old fellow contentedly sitting by waiting for his pot to boil. Art critics have pronounced the painting worth $600.00, but it is offered at $350.00.

Blizzard of 1888: Southington, Connecticut; postcard, early 1900s.

Southington, Connecticut. The Old Leather Man's cave/rock shelter was near D. R. Sloper Pond, east of the slaughterhouse (center). He had other shelters on Ragged Mountain and Short Mountain in Berlin. Baker and Tilden, Atlas of Hartford County, Connecticut, 1869.

TERRY'S ART GALLERY,

43 North Main, cor. Laurel Street,

A FEW YARDS WEST OF DEPOT.

Greenhouses at Residence on West St.

PHOTOGRAPHS AND ALL KINDS OF PICTURES,

Of the Highest Class taken in the best manner. Old pictures copied
and finished in Ink or Colors, in the most artistic styles.

Picture Frames, Carved, Fancy and Art Goods.

Advertisement, Bristol Directory, 1888–1889.

*The Old Leather Man, painted by Charles C. Benham in 1888; postcard
of painting, early 1900s. Benham, a New Haven artist and woodwork
designer, painted this view after an 1885 photograph by James Rodgers of
the Old Leather Man sitting in front of his shelter on Pond Rock above
Lake Saltonstall in East Haven. Benham's portrait was nearly life-sized.
When Barney S. Kirdzik bought the Forestville Grill (Center Street,
Forestville), the painting came with it. For many years, the portrait looked
down on the restaurant's patrons. In 1940, Mr. Kirdzik sold the painting
to the owners of the North Main Street Tavern in Bristol. At some point,
the portrait disappeared, and its present location is unknown.*

*Wooden tools said to have been the Old Leather Man's snow shovels.
Found by James Fish of East Street, Southington, Connecticut, in an area
where the Leather Man had built a shelter. Leroy W. Foote collection.*

Deep River New Era, Friday, March 23, 1888

The Old Leather Man

An oil painting of the old Leather Man in front of his
hut in Branford is on exhibition in W. A. Terry's window
in Bristol. The scene is near Lake Saltonstall in a forest
of large trees by a small stream. The painting is by
C. C. Benham of New Haven.

Deep River New Era, Friday, March 23, 1888

LOCAL

The Old Leather Man remained in a cave in the eastern part
of Southington during the storm, but has since emerged,
and commenced his tramp again. He went through this
village on Tuesday afternoon about 4 o'clock.

Deep River New Era, Friday, March 23, 1888

ESSEX

The old Leather Man passed through this place Wednesday. He was behind his schedule time.

Meriden Journal, Wednesday, March 28, 1888

The Leather Man is on his rounds again. The blizzard delayed him only five days.

Deep River New Era, Friday, March 30, 1888
ESSEX

The old Leather Man on his last tramp through this town failed for the first time in years to stop at his accustomed place for his lunch. He took a different route from what he usually takes. He was seen Wednesday between Essex and Deep River, and the probabilities are he took the back road or followed the railroad track, knowing it would be more free from snow drifts.

Penny Press, Monday, April 23, 1888

The Leather Man passed through Staddle Hill today, took dinner at Mrs. Fisher's and wrote some letters in a notebook for John G. Palmer, at the Arrowanna mills.[9] That is a new kind of notice of the Leather Man.

Penny Press, Tuesday, April 24, 1888

The leather man has an appetite. When he partook of refreshments at Mrs. Fisher's, Staddle Hill, he drank three quarts of coffee, and had solids to match. He refused to talk except by a word. It was intended to have a photograph of him, but as he was a day behind time that scheme failed. The leather man is due at Staddle Hill once a month.

New Haven Daily Palladium, Tuesday, May 1, 1888
NORTH HAVEN

The Leather man passed through here as the 1:58 p.m. train south was at the depot, and caused some excitement among the passengers, to whom he was apparently a new sight. He was on time, his last trip through here being March 24.

9. Palmer's mill manufactured mosquito netting and hammocks. Today, Palmer Field occupies its former site.

Arrowwanna Mills, Middletown, Connecticut, 1864.

Morning Journal and Courier, Tuesday, May 1, 1888

The Leather Man

The old Leather man visited I. W. Beach's house at Forestville last Friday and regaled himself with a breakfast made up as follows: One quart of coffee, a plate of crackers, three slices of bread, three pickles, three crullers, one pint of peanuts, two cigars. It being Friday he refused meat, but loaded his gripsack with a good supply. He also refused eggs and oranges. Mr. Beach talked with him in regard to the blizzard. He said he did not suffer much but could not travel.

Deep River New Era, Friday, June 8, 1888

The Leather Man's Love
CONNECTICUT'S MYSTERIOUS
WANDERER SPEAKS AT LAST
Bridgeport, Conn., May 26.—A more romantic, weird and strangely complex life has never been accredited to

Depot and post office, North Haven, Connecticut; postcard, early 1900s. Leroy F. Roberts collection.

North Haven, Connecticut. F. W. Beers, Ellis, and Soule, Atlas of New Haven County, Connecticut, *1868.*

man than that lived by Randolph Mossey, well known in Eastern Conn. as "The Leather Man."

The nomadic characteristics of this strange individual have caused him to be a subject for comment for many years, but no one ever solved the mystery surrounding him. Who he was, where his home or what his condition or circumstances in life, no one could fathom until this week when a *Journal* reporter had the good luck to penetrate the chrysalis that for twenty-nine years has secretly hid the secrets of Mossey's life and the cause of his being a long wanderer on the face of earth.

On the morning of May 21[10] the *Journal* man sauntered over to the Naugatuck junction, a small switch station just across the Housatonic River, in the town of Milford, with a view of meeting "The Leather Man." It was expected that the silent and solitary wanderer would pass this point on that date, for he seldom has failed to appear at certain places at regular intervals. Sure enough, at 11:34 a.m. the strange-looking creature was observed coming slowly down the Naugatuck Railroad.

Crossing the Consolidated road to the south, the "Leather Man" followed the foot-path that led to a spring of cool water mid-way between the old Washington Bridge and the railroad bridge. There he sat

down to rest after quenching his thirst. It was there that he was approached by the *Journal* representative; who after an almost hopeless effort, succeeding in inducing the old man to speak. For a full half hour he had simply used his head in reply to interrogatories. Finally he said:

"Vy you speak ze many question?"

"I want you to say something about yourself," was the *Journal* man's reply.

"Oh, out; I have nosing to say."

Then it occurred to the reporter to continue the conversation in French, and the effect was electrical, in less than five minutes the confidence of the old Frenchman was won, and for the first time the secrets of this strange person were revealed.

Rudolph[11] Mossey, better known as the "Leather Man," is a native of Rouen, a small town about ninety miles northwest of Paris. Twenty-nine years ago he was the happy husband of a beautiful wife, to whom he was devotedly attached. He earned a good living at boot and shoe making, and gave her all the comforts his earnings could supply. But, eight months after his marriage a traitor in the disguise of a friend entered his home, and after winning the affections of his wife fled with her to America. The blow was a severe one, from which Mossey never recovered. He sold his effects and, although unaware of the whereabouts of the runaway

10. On May 21, 1888, the *Journal* reporter could not have met the Old Leather Man at Naugatuck Junction in Milford. See "Excerpt from a Time Table of the Old Leather Man."

11. Other references identify him as Randolph, not Rudolph.

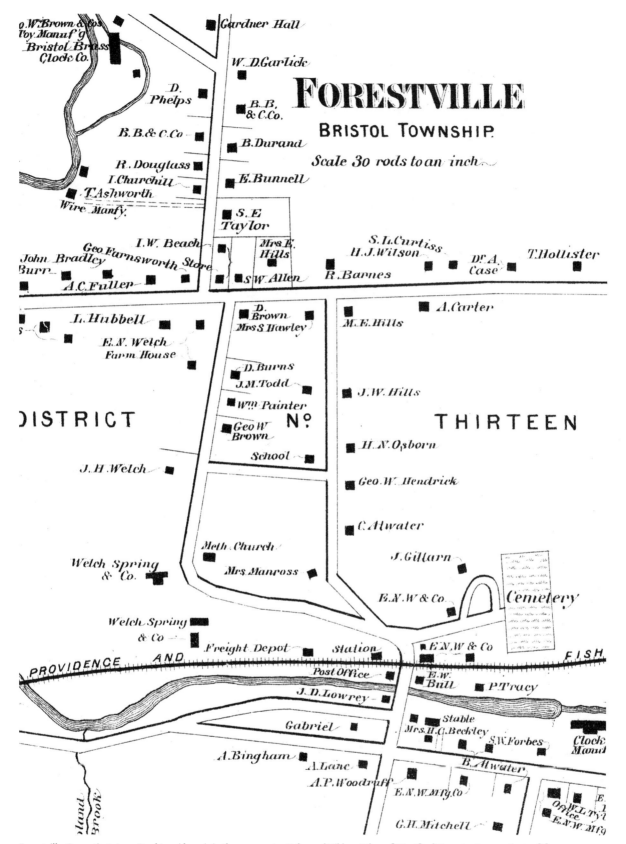

Forrestville, Connecticut. Isaac Beach's residence is in the upper center. Baker and Tilden, Atlas of Hartford County, Connecticut, 1869.

Montage of Washington Bridges, Milford, Connecticut ("1868–1921; 1808–1867; New Bridge 1921"); postcard, circa 1921.

wife, he came to America determined to give the country a thorough search. After three years of tireless inquiry he was rewarded by meeting the man who had ruined his life. It was at the corner of Chapel and Church street, New Haven, that the meeting occurred, and, like a sleuth hound, Mossey followed his betrayer step by step until he entered a house on Crown street. There Mossey thought to find his wife, and bouncing up the steps he attempted to enter every room in the house. He was seized by the inmates, who imagined him to be insane. One of his captors was the man that had stolen his wife. A dramatic scene followed the recognition, and during the excitement Mossey learned his wife had been dead only a short time. Then a terrible conflict between the two Frenchmen took place. Mossey was fighting to kill, and had it not been for the arrival of help he would have had his revenge. But he was overpowered and compelled to witness the escape of his enemy, who made haste to join a Connecticut regiment, and at the battle of Fredericksburg lost an arm.

Two years later Mossey met the destroyer of his happiness again. He noticed the armless sleeve and imagining the cause had not the heart to shoot down a maimed and defenseless soldier. He made himself known, however, and though he was ragged and dirty

his enemy fell at his feet and implored him not to kill. Mossey gave him his life on one condition: that he should be shown the grave of his wife. His request was willingly complied with and Mossey's heart softened when he beheld a neat slab at the head of her grave. Desiring to be left alone with his dear, he remained for two days and nights beside the tomb, and would have died there had he not been forcibly ejected from the cemetery. Later Mossey begun working at his trade, and while thus engaged learned that his wife had lived in different places while the companion of the man with whom she eloped, and having lost all ambition he finally made himself a complete suit of available leather scraps and started on his ceaseless tramp, a heartbroken wanderer with only one desire, to some day rest beside his wife. Semi-annually he visits her grave and each place where she lived, going over the same route taken by her. He rests an hour or two at each place, and patches his costume with pieces of leather that he finds in scrap barrels or by the wayside.

During the terrible blizzard of March 12 the wind tore the fastenings from Mossey's coat and the pelting snow fell upon his breast and froze his flesh.

Mossey is fifty-five years old, although he looks to be seventy. For twenty-three years he has tramped through

Eastern Connecticut. He would not divulge the name of the man who wrecked his life nor would he tell where his wife is buried, but said: "I can forgive the man, but can never forget. He will put my bones by her side and then I will be content."

EXCERPT FROM A TIMETABLE
OF THE LEATHER MAN[12]
S. A. Hale, of Signal Tower No. 20, Naugatuck Junction, Consolidated road, kept a record of his trips as he passed Naugatuck Junction from 1883 until he made last trip at 1:20 p. m. Tuesday, February 26, 1889.

The Record as he passed Naugatuck Junction, Conn., Going West.

Date	Time of Day	Days Out
1888		
Tuesday, January 10	2:29 p.m.	36
Thursday, February 16	1:55 p.m.	37
Monday, March 26	2:49 p.m.	39
Wednesday, May 2	3:05 p.m.	37
Thursday, June 7	11:14 p.m.	36
Sunday, July 15	9:48 p.m.	38

Morning Journal and Courier, Tuesday, August 21, 1888, North Haven

The old leather man was found lying on the sidewalk near Mr. Harvey Leete's residence Sunday morning, and evidence conclusive that he had passed the night there. He was furnished food by Mr. Leete's family and proceeded on his way.

Penny Press, Thursday, August 23, 1888

Leather Man Again
Frank Wetherell[13] has in his possession an excellent photograph of the somewhat celebrated leather man, who for the past 20 years has traveled all over the west-

Harvey Leete's residence on Broadway, North Haven, Connecticut, late 1800s. Courtesy of the North Haven Historical Society.

ern part of the state. The picture was taken by an amateur operator in Middlefield, and represents him eating some food given by kindly disposed people. The leather man is dressed in bootlegs cut up and roughly sewed together with strips of leather and fashioned into garments. A cancer has made its appearance upon the lower lip of the old man, and if it is left with its malignant growth unchecked, it is certain that his days are numbered. He refused money offered him, and striking his breast indicated he was plentifully supplied, to prove which he drew out of his pockets about $7.

—*New London Telegraph.*

Bristol Weekly Press, Thursday, September 20, 1888
FORESTVILLE

The "leather man" passed through here Sunday afternoon at about 4:30 o'clock, two days behind time. He is looking bad and his lip is about eaten away by cancer.

Penny Press, Friday, September 21, 1888
STATE NEWS

Mr. Moore, photographer, went out to Fisher's Mill, Staddle Hill, Wednesday, and photographed the Leather

12. The complete time table is in the New Haven *Evening Register*, Monday, April 8, 1889.

13. Frank Wetherell was Mrs. Amy Guy's son from her first marriage.

The Old Leather Man, taken in May 1888 by Dr. Rust, an amateur photographer in Middlefield, Connecticut, at Mrs. Amy Guy's residence on Higby Road. Leroy W. Foote collection.

The Old Leather Man, taken in 1888 by photographer Frederick J. Moore at Fisher's Mill in Staddle Hill, Middletown, Connecticut.

Man. He obtained eight negatives, which are splendid. The old man sat quietly and facial lines and every patch in his garments are clearly defined. The old man has a terrible cancer on his lip and is nearing the dark shadow. He is in the 35th year of his wandering through this district. Mr. Moore, at his photo studio, in Middletown, has copies of the Old Leather Man for sale at 25 cents each.

Evening News, Monday, October 1, 1888

The old leather man was in *Westville* last week, but much changed in appearance and some people failed to recognize him. He wore a felt hat and woolen trousers. The New Haven Union says: "But the same old coat still hangs in unfashionable folds from his broad shoulders. But it shows signs of hard usage and unless the wearer can conceive some way of immediate repair it will necessarily have to follow the trousers and hat and be relegated to the things that were." He refused to talk, though several persons tried to get an explanation of the change in his dress.

The Old Leather Man, taken in 1888 by photographer Frederick J. Moore at Fisher's Mill in Staddle Hill, Middletown, Connecticut. Leroy W. Foote collection.

Brewster Standard, Friday evening, October 5, 1888

When the "Old Leather Man" passed through Terryville a few days ago it was noticed that his lower lip was badly eaten away with cancer. A physician who saw him says it is only a matter of time when his tramping will come to an end forever.

Evening News, Tuesday, October 9, 1888

The last time the leather man passed through New Milford he took dinner, as he has done for years, with Horace Allen. Mr. Allen noticed a bad looking sore on his lip, which was distorted by it, and urged him to see a doctor about it. At Terryville, recently, the disease was seen to be cancer, and its work was already terribly advanced. Will not the authorities put the poor fellow somewhere before cold weather comes? He will suffer and die alone unless kindly force is used to provide him home and shelter.

Hartford Courant, Thursday, October 11, 1888

The Old Leather Man

HIS HOPELESS DISEASE—THE
PROPRIETY OF NON-INTERFERENCE

The "old leather man" has become a good deal of a chestnut, but he is an interesting character all the same, and it is worth while to question the suggestion that is made in his supposed interest by the *Danbury News*. That paper says he has a cancer on the face that was noticed some time ago and has made considerable progress. Then it adds: "Will not the authorities put the poor fellow somewhere before cold weather comes! He will suffer and die alone unless kindly force is used to provide him home and shelter." Here is where it seems possible to make a great mistake. The man finds his only enjoyment in his absolutely free life. If he were shut up in what people generally would call comfort there is little doubt that he would fret and pine. He might be told that he could report at any time at some place and

Main Street, looking east, Terryville, Connecticut; postcard, early 1900s.

be provided with food, shelter and such care as he might need, but to take him before he desired would be mere cruelty. And if he prefers to trudge on to the last and then lie down and die by himself as he has lived, who should interfere? It may be that he would pass more easily in that way than surrounded by all appliances of medical treatment and wholly shut off from the way of life he has chosen and which he has followed so many years.

[Unidentified newspaper,[14] probably the Woodbury Reporter], Woodbury, Connecticut, 1888

The old Leather man passed here Sunday, October 21, at his usual hour of noon. He is evidently suffering terribly from cancer of the lip.

Penny Press, Tuesday, October 30, 1888

The Shadows Increase
The Old Leather man passed through Staddle Hill Saturday and made a call at Fisher's house. Mr. Moore obtained some large photos of him while there. The can-

14. From an old scrapbook in the Woodbury Library.

cer on his lip is now double in surface to what it was a month ago. It is evident that the end of the "Old Leather Man" draweth nigh.

Bristol Weekly Press, Thursday, November 1, 1888
FORESTVILLE

The "leather man" ate a good meal at the house of I. W. Beach last week, remaining an hour and a half. He was sociable and had Mr. Beach examine his neck, which is swollen from the cancer on his face. It is thought that he will not make many more trips. The report that he has cast off his leather hat and coat is not true.

Penny Press, Thursday, November 1, 1888

The Humane Society After Him
Moore, the photographer, has secured two more negatives of the old leather man and has them on exhibition in McKee's Drug store window.

He was at the residence of Mr. Fisher in Staddle Hill, Saturday and partook of his rations as usual. The cancer on his lip is fast taking the old man away and it is a question if he stands it the coming winter. However, the Humane Society are considering his case and it is

The Old Leather Man, taken in 1888 by photographer Frederick J. Moore at Fisher's Mill in Staddle Hill, Middletown, Connecticut.

safe to say the next time he comes this way he will be taken in charge of and placed in some place for the winter for his safety.

Penny Press, Monday, December 3, 1888

His Noted Career Ended—The Leather Man Arrested This Morning

THE HUMANE SOCIETY TAKE HIM
IN CHARGE AND HE IS TAKEN TO
HARTFORD HOSPITAL FOR TREATMENT.
AFTER YEARS OF WANDERING AND
SOLITUDE HE IS TAKEN CHARGE OF BY
THE STATE—UNEQUALED IN HISTORY.

This noon Chief of police Chapman and Agent Thrall, of the Humane Society, went to Staddle Hill for the purpose of taking in charge and arresting an old vagrant, who is well known as the "Old Leather Man." The authorities of the law were advised about what time this strange piece of humanity would be in this section and this morning was the time he passed a given point in

Staddle Hill. For years now he has been stopping at the residence of Mr. Fisher, the miller, on his trips through these parts and receiving his supply of victuals that were tendered him by the kind-hearted lady of the house. He made his appearance there about a month ago and several fine photographs were obtained of him by Moore, the photographer. The attention of the Humane Society was then called to his condition, but he had gone his way before the necessary steps could be taken to make him a prisoner. For nearly a year now the old man has been suffering from a cancer on his lip and it is steadily eating out his life's blood; so much so that the Humane Society have concluded that he is not a fit person to roam at large and thus his arrest this morning in Staddle Hill.

The Leather Man, as he is termed, has been a familiar character of curiosity for some years now and his stated visits through different towns of the state have made him almost an everyday person to a great many people. In years gone by and when he first visited these parts, he was brighter than he is now and his appearance was not to be wondered at, considering the mode he pursued to gain a livelihood. But age has told its story on the old man and he will be safer housed in some hospital for treatment than to roam about the woods and over the mountains, living as he has done, in caves and obscure places; for the disease that he is afflicted with, it would be a question if he could face the wintry blast of the approaching winter.

Some, who have endeavored to ascertain the old man's history, claim he is of French descent and that in his youth he was a member of one of the first families in France. He became infatuated with a handsome young French lady, but through some unknown cause the match was broken off and the leather man, as he is now termed, sought refuge for his broken heart in this enlightened land. He pursued the life he has followed for years now, that of tramping through Connecticut, having his regular resorts where he obtained his eatables and resting at night in places known only to himself. The story goes that the young and beautiful French lady whom he adored, went insane after his departure, because she could not have the man she loved and was incarcerated in an asylum, a raving maniac. It is said that even well to do Frenchmen have visited this country and interviewed the old man and tried to persuade him to return to his native country, where a fortune was in waiting, but he would not listen to the appeal made, in the meantime preferring his mode of life which he had sought after being smitten by his first love.

In the summer it was no uncommon sight to see him roaming through the woods, apparently happy and it might be added that he was not a pleasant person to meet, providing the casual observer was not acquainted with the leather suit and its quaint appearance.

Hartford Times, Monday evening, December 3, 1888

"The Old Leather Man"
SPECIAL TO THE HARTFORD TIMES

MIDDLETOWN, DECEMBER 3
The person known as "the Old Leather Man" made his appearance in this place today. He is nearly dead from the effects of a large cancer upon his lips. He was arrested by R. L. DeZeng, agent of the Humane Society, and taken to Hartford Hospital this afternoon.

Patient Records, Hartford Hospital, Monday, December 3, 1888, from the Hamilton Archives Health Science Library

No. 13096, Date: 12-3-1888, Name: Zach Bovelat, Residence: Middletown,
Nativity: France, Occupation: None, Age: 55, Sex: M, Color: W,
Habits T (Temperate),
Page: 4274, Disease: Epithelioma of lip, Result of treatment: Eloped
Discharged: 12-3-1888, Name of Responsible Party: Charity

Middletown Herald, Tuesday, December 4, 1888

Zack Boveliat
THE OLD LEATHER MAN REFUSES TO BE TAKEN TO THE HOSPITAL AND ESCAPES
Agent DeZeng and the Humane Society learned three new facts regarding the old leather man yesterday. First that his name is Zacharias Boveliat: second that he was born in France and third that he is quite spry when he chooses to be.

For over 30 years Boveliat has tramped through this section of the country, living in caves and living on the kind charity of families along the line of his tramp. Last winter during the blizzard the lower portion of his face was frozen and in August a malignant cancer appeared on his lower lip. Agent DeZeng saw him a few months ago and decided that the interest of humanity would be subserved by placing him in some comfortable place.

Sunday afternoon word was received that he had passed the Highland house in Westfield. Yesterday morning Mrs. Amy Guy of Middletown sent word that he had called at her home. Agent DeZeng, State Agent Thrall, Chief Chapman and Dr. Sage went out to Hiram Fisher's.[15] About 1 o'clock, Boveliat appeared and entered Fisher's kitchen, as has been his custom in the

15. Richard L. DeZeng of Middletown, Dwight W. Thrall of Hartford, Middletown Police Chief Jedediah C. Chapman, and Fredrick Sage, homeopathic physician, of Middletown. Hiram Fisher was the son of John and Susan Fisher, who owned the grist mill in the Stadde Hill district of Middletown.

Hartford Hospital. The name of the person who supplied information for the hospital's form is unknown.
Courtesy of the Hamilton Archives Health Science Library, Hartford Hospital.

past. Dr. Sage was called in, examined his lip and decided that something must be done or the cancer would kill the old man within a short time. After Mr. and Mrs. Fisher and Mr. DeZeng had talked with him a short time, after promising to give him his liberty in the spring, he consented to come with DeZeng and Thrall. While he was in this city hundreds of persons called at Bent's livery stable and saw him.

While on his way to Hartford in a team, Boveliat attempted to brain both DeZeng and Thrall with a club, which he carried. He was soon disarmed and then he attempted to jump from the wagon, but the two humane gentlemen succeeded in getting him to the hospital where he was placed in charge of the officials. It was here that they learned his name. When he was asked if he was a French Canadian he was very indignant and said he was a native of France.

Shortly after DeZeng and Thrall left the hospital, Boveliat escaped from the institution and this morning was seen going towards the south on the Connecticut Valley track.

This town will have to bear one half of the expense

for his care and the state the balance. If he develops traits of insanity as is expected, he will be placed in the insane asylum. When he attacked the humane agents yesterday, his eye fairly glistened with fire. He has nearly lost the use of his voice and talks in a guttural and almost unintelligible tone of voice.

Penny Press, Tuesday, December 4, 1888

The Leather Man Again

HE ESCAPES FROM THE HARTFORD
HOSPITAL LAST EVENING

As stated, in the press of yesterday the old Leather Man was conveyed to the Hartford Hospital by State Agent Thrall, of the Humane Society and Agent R. L. DeZeng, of this city. On his journey to Hartford, over the rough roads, he complained about his face hurting him. After his journey he was quietly placed in the room assigned him in the spacious building. The officers left and he was turned over to the authorities in charge. He must have escaped from the hospital shortly after his con-

Union Station, Middletown, Connecticut; postcard, early 1900s. Leroy F. Roberts collection.

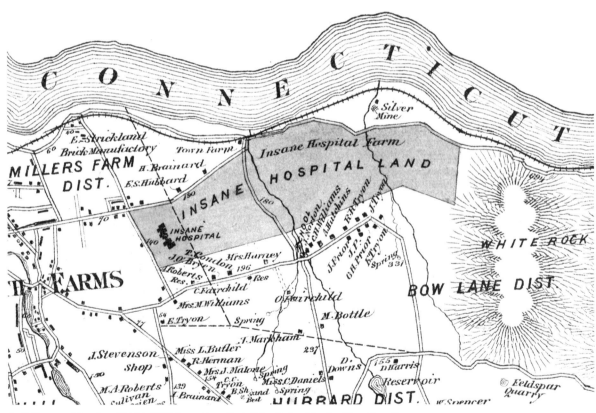

South Farms and Bow Lane District, Middletown, Connecticut. Valley Railroad tracks at top, Town Farm
(also called the Poor House) at upper center, White Rocks at right. The Old Leather Man had a number of shelters in this area.
Leroy F. Roberts Collection, from F. W. Beers, Atlas of Middlesex County, Connecticut, 1874.

Humane Society Agent Richard DeZeng, of Middletown, Connecticut. Courtesy of the Middlesex County Historical Society.

finement, for he reached this city at an early hour this morning[16] and proceeded down the Conn. Valley railroad track at a lively rate of speed, considering his advanced age. He was noticed by several bystanders at Union depot, but he paid no attention to anyone, merely stopping occasionally to pick up a stray cigar stump, or quid of tobacco. Several started in pursuit of him, merely to talk with him, but he would have nothing to say. He was stopped at the Poor House crossing by a lady and gentleman and talked a few minutes. He was later accosted by two men from the city, who had driven down the road ahead of him, but he would say nothing, merely pointing to the white rocks in the distance and muttering to himself. How he escaped from the asylum is not known, but it is probable that he walked out while no one was looking and continued his course down the river. He is now on his old trail and ere this, likely, is safely housed in one of his curious places of abode. Agent De Zeng was anxious to have the old fellow recaptured this morning, but the police stated they had no business to interfere with him and thus he meandered unmolested. It is the general belief that he should be left to wander as he has done for 35 years now. As he is a burden to no one; is inoffensive in his way and prefers the wilds of outdoor life to that of being housed up in some place for treatment for the deadly cancer is working on him. As he has roamed, so let him roam and save the town and state the necessity of caring for him.

16. His journey from Hartford to Middletown was approximately eighteen miles.

Hartford Times, Tuesday evening, December 4, 1888

Again on the Tramp

THE "OLD LEATHER MAN" SUDDENLY
LEAVES THE HOSPITAL

A special to the *Times* from Middletown, yesterday afternoon announced the action of the Connecticut Humane Society in arresting the "Old Leather Man" and the intentions to place him under the care of the physicians in the Hartford Hospital. This action was considered humane, as the wanderer is suffering from a malignant cancer on the lip, which has eaten the greater portion of one side of his chin. This was caused by his exposure last winter, when his face and portions of his body were frozen.[17] For thirty years he has tramped over this state and the Humane Society has not interfered, although the agents have been appealed to. He was harmless, always had plenty to eat and enjoyed his mode of life. Now the conditions have changed and after consulting legal authorities it was considered within the province of the society's agents to restrain him and care for him during the few months before his certain death.

Agent DeZeng, of Middletown, was advised of his whereabouts a day or two ago and with Agent Dwight Thrall, of this city, found him at the house of Mr. Fisher, at Staddle Hill, yesterday. He accompanied the officer without opposition and the Middletown insane asylum being full the old traveler was brought to this city by carriage, arriving about 4 o'clock.

Once during the trip he made resistance and attempted to use his staff on Agent Thrall, but he was quieted.

Arriving at the hospital he was placed in the care of the officials, the Humane Society's agents asking that he be restrained if he attempted to escape. They also advised that his leather suit be replaced by a suit of clothing. Hardly had his captors left when he demanded that he be allowed to go. The hospital officials having no power to keep him against his will, permitted him to take his leather "grip" and depart. When the agents were notified it was too dark to make a search for the man and hence nothing was done.

The "Leather Man" was anxious to pick up his jour-

17. More likely, the cancer resulted from chewing and smoking tobacco from the cigar and cigarette butts he picked up.

ney where it had been interrupted and he headed for Middletown, which city he reached about 7 o'clock this morning. He was walking on the railroad track and was on his way to one of his resorts, a cave midway between Middletown and Higganum. The overhanging rock is thatch with boughs, straw and mud, with a small opening and here he spends a portion of his time when not on his tramps. The Humane Society is undecided what action to take in the matter. Certain it is that some one should care for the suffering man. His condition is pitiable and the disease is beyond hope of recovery.

Hartford Courant, Tuesday, December 4, 1888

The "Old Leather Man"

PLACED IN THE HOSPITAL BY THE HUMANE SOCIETY, HE REFUSES TO REMAIN

HIS PITIFUL CONDITION

The "old leather man," whose wanderings have frequently been noted in these columns, has of late followed a route, which led him through Meriden and Middletown at regular intervals, about a month apart. On these journeys he has stopped at the house of Mr. Fisher on Staddle Hill for refreshment. Some months ago Mr. Fisher called the attention of Mr. De Zeng, agent of the Connecticut Humane society at Middletown, to the old traveler's deplorable condition and suggested that the society endeavor to do something for him. Mr. De Zeng ascertained that in his regular round the leather man would arrive at Mr. Fisher's yesterday. Accordingly, yesterday forenoon, Messrs De Zeng and Thrall, of the Humane society, accompanied by the town physician and chief of police, droved out to Mr. Fisher's.

The leather man had not arrived and while they were waiting for him a telephone message was sent to the state hospital for the insane, asking if he could be received there. The superintendent replied that they could not receive him at present. He soon arrived at Mr. Fisher's and the physician examined him. He found that a malignant cancer had eaten away the lower part of his chin and mouth on the left side, producing a depression of nearly two inches and that a large swelling had developed under the chin on the same side during the past month. Mr. De Zeng gained the old man's confidence and he finally consented to get into the buggy with him and Mr. Thrall and was driven to Middletown. The Hartford Hospital authorities were telephoned too and replied that they would take him immediately. The selectmen of Middletown gave an order for his admission to the Hospital. A carriage was procured and Messrs De Zeng and Thrall started for Hartford with their patient. During the latter part of the ride he was very uneasy and endeavored to escape, but was safely delivered at the hospital. Mr. De Zeng cautioned the attendants to take his leather suit from him and keep a sharp watch on him, as he would probably try to get away. Soon after the hospital announced that he had made his escape only a few minutes after their departure.

In taking this step the officers and agents of the Humane Society were acting only for the old man's good. This diseased condition of his face undoubtedly results from its having been frozen and exposure to another winter would probably be fatal to him. He is likely at any time to become a charge upon some town. The attorney for the society was already of the opinion that the proposed action was legally justifiable. But the nomadic habits of this strange being will not brook restraint. He will now probably change his route, but seems likely to pursue his vagabond life until stricken down by his final sickness.

Bridgeport Evening Farmer, Tuesday, December 4, 1888

STATE HAPPENINGS

The "Old Leather Man" was arrested in Middletown on Monday by Chief of Police Chapman and an agent of the Connecticut Humane Society. The harmless old tramp was taken to the Hartford hospital, and it is possible that something authentic may soon be obtained about his life and history. For years he has tramped through sections of Connecticut, receiving food from sympathizing strangers, and sleeping in caves and places known only to himself. His singular suit of leather has given him a wide reputation. A cancer has been growing upon his lip for one year, and it will probably cause his death within a year.

Many romantic stories have been published about the old man, but it is probable that his mysterious life has not yet been truthfully presented. He has not yet told any one the story of his life and, though often asked, has always been silent.

Hartford Evening Post,
Wednesday, December 5, 1888
MIDDLETOWN

The old leather man is like Jeff Davis. He wants to be let alone.

The old leather man stepped off towards Higganum quite lively yesterday. "No pent up Utica contracts his powers." He roams the state at large.

Bristol Weekly Press, Thursday, December 6, 1888
FORESTVILLE

The leather man passed through here last Friday. He looked much worse than last time. His mouth is in bad shape.

Bridgeport Morning News,
Tuesday, December 11, 1888

The Leather Man's Lucre

So many people are acquainted either by sight or hearsay with the famous leather man who perambulates about the state and keeps a schedule of time in his wanderings, that they will be interested to learn that the old and quaint pedestrian is reported to be worth considerable money. We have it from pretty good authority that the ancient wonder has deposited $35,000 with a friend at different periods and seems to be pretty well fixed in this world's goods despite his leathery and old habiliments.

New Haven Evening Register,
Tuesday, December 11, 1888

The Old Leather Man
COLD AND HUNGER FINALLY
COMPEL HIM TO ASK FOR CHARITY

North Haven, Conn., Dec. 11. The "old leather man" about whom so much has been recently written, appears to have departed from his usual custom of holding no communion with his fellow man:

Shortly before noon Sunday a cold rain was falling when a knock sounded on the door of James F. Barnard of this place. Mr. Barnard answered the knock and there, dripping with rain, covered with mud and shivering from the cold, was the old leather man, a most pitiable sight.

He was taken in out of the storm and much welcomed. He appeared to take comfort sitting close to the fire and eagerly accepted hot coffee, bread, pie and cake. After a generous meal of these, he drank six large bowls of milk. He watched every movement of those about him with evident suspicion.

While the old man was engaged in appeasing his hunger, the family had an exceptionally good opportunity of making a study of him. He appeared to be about 50 years of age and a close inspection showed that at one time he must have been a fine looking man. He has a high, commanding forehead and his hair, which was matted by exposure and neglect, was dark brown in color and very fine. It was only slightly tinged with gray. His eyes, which were large and dark-blue in color, have a wandering and innocent expression. His clothing was made of leather, stitched with thongs. He wore a long coat, with pockets inside and out. His boots had thick soles. A soldier's cap, with a leather visor, completed his costume and he carried two bags, one of which was filled with old leather bootlegs.

The physical condition of the man was pitiable and shows intense suffering. On his lower lip was a malignant cancer, which has eaten away a large portion of the lip. Under the jaw is a swelling as large as a medium size orange. His whole appearance is one to evoke pity and as he sat and ate the food offered to him, he was a sight to be remembered. He dried his mouth with one of the

Former residence of Mr. and Mrs. James F. Barnard, 53 Maple Avenue, North Haven, Connecticut. Photo by D. W. DeLuca, 2002.

rags and when a member of the family offered him a napkin, he examined it curiously, shook his head and handed it back. He was offered a pipe, tobacco and matches, but refused them. He also declined to talk and when he had finished eating, arose as if to leave the house. When told that he might remain as long as he wished, he pointed up the road and with an emphatic gesture said:

"Must go; must go!"

With these words he left the house and continued on his mysterious tramp.

Penny Press, Wednesday, December 12, 1888

Wanted in a Museum

MELHAM & WILSON WANT THE LEATHER MAN
Jules Bourglay, known as the "Leather Man" is coming into prominence again, from the fact that a New York museum is willing to take the old man, providing he is in good health and would exhibit himself for a large salary annually. It is evident the proprietors of the museum, Melham & Wilson, have seen more or less about the "Leather Man" in newspapers, the first report having appeared in the press about the time he was arrested and taken to Hartford Hospital. The letter in question is written to Chief of Police Chapman in this city and is as follows:

> Dear Sir; Can you give address of Jules Borglay, the "Leather Man," and information as whether he is in a fit condition, as far as health is concerned and whether he would, in your opining, be willing to place himself on exhibition for a good salary; by so doing you will greatly oblige.
> Yours Truly,
> Melham & Wilson.

Chief Chapman says he don't know whether the old man would accept or not, and that he had got through looking after or bothering with him. After escaping from the hospital some two weeks ago, he took his old course down the valley again and Monday night reached West Haven, where he ate ravenously and would not say anything, only that he was going on. He will continue his course as far as Stamford, thence up the Naugatuck valley and through this section again, arriving here about the second week in January.

Letter from Mrs James Barnard to Meehan and Wilson's Globe Museum

North Haven, Conn., Jan. 4, 1889
Messrs. Meehan and Wilson,
Gentlemen; Yours in reference to the Leather Man received. I don't think, as far as I can learn there is any possibility of getting him for exhibition. He either cannot or will not talk. He has traveled this state thirty years and his route is so regular that you can tell to an hour when he will pass. He appears here every four weeks. No one knows where he stays nights, but suppose in the woods. He never begs nor stops at houses. He never was known to knock at a door before he came to ours. He would not talk to us, but we talked to him and he looked as if he knew what we said. His clothes would make the feature of a museum; pants, vest, coat, hat and a sack, all made of bootlegs sewed together with thongs of leather like belt lacing. The leather bag was full of pieces of leather and a short-handled axe. Some say he is French and his name is Jean Bogeaureau, but no one knows. We have his picture, which was taken by a man following him all day with a team, until he got a chance unseen to take it. I send you a copy.

He is due here one week from today and I will talk to him and see if he will talk; all he said before was "must go," which he said plain enough.

He will not live long in all probability, as the cancer on his face is very bad.
Yours truly,
Mrs. James F. Barnard,
North Haven, Conn.[18]

18. From *Life of the Mysterious Leather Man, the Wandering Hermit of Connecticut and New York*, by A. B. Stewart, published by Meehan & Wilson's Globe Museum, 298 Bowery, New York City, 1889.

Part IV   1889

Bristol Herald, Thursday, January 10, 1889, Forestville

The Old Leather Man passed through this village last Sunday afternoon notwithstanding the rain while it drizzled down in a most uncomfortable manner. As usual he stopped at the house of Mr. I. W. Beach where he was fed and where owing to his horrible appearance and the probability that he is unable at any time to close his pilgrimage, a determined effort was made by Mr. Beach to find out something about him. He was furnished with pencil and paper and requested to write his name. He took the pencil and made the figures from one to nine, inclusive, but beyond this nothing could be got out of him, he used the word France several times to convey the idea that he was a native of that country, but no coaxing could get him to tell his name. He cannot eat solid food owing to the cancer on his lip, which is badly eaten away and his throat is swollen from ear to ear.

Penny Press, Tuesday, January 15, 1889
CLINTON

The Old Leather Man passed through here bound west, Sunday morning at 11:45. He stopped at Eben's and was fed as usual. He is looking very badly, the cancer on his lip has eaten away a large part of it and shows signs of breaking out his neck under his lower jaw.

Bristol Herald, Thursday, January 17, 1889

The last time the Old Leather Man passed through Polkville,[1] Mr. Samuel W. Steele stopped him and offered him some money, but the old fellow refused it and only took a quantity of food that Mr. Steele urged upon him. Mr. Steele said he looked very badly indeed on account of the cancer, which has eaten away the greater portion of his lower lip.

1. Polkville is a village in Bristol, Connecticut.

Bristol Weekly Press, Thursday, January 24, 1889

It is said that the cancer on the "old leather man's" lip has become so serious that he can only eat food soaked in coffee and then it hurts him so that tears run down his cheek while eating. It is probable that he will be unable to continue his lonely tramp much longer.

Evening News, Friday, January 25, 1889

The Leather Man in Redding

The Leather Man was in Redding and called early in the morning at the residence of Dr. J. H. Benedict, where he asked for a breakfast.

He was readily recognized by Mrs. Benedict from his leather clothing, and she invited him into the kitchen. As Mrs. Benedict can speak French she soon learned his wants, which were simply coffee, and she furnished him with all he desired. He drank the full of two large bowls, into each of which he put a teacupful of sugar.

He explained that he was unable to partake of solid food on account of his cancer, which prevented chewing. He conversed for a short time with Mrs. Benedict in French, until she asked him of his antecedents and

The Old Leather Man, photographer and location unknown.
Leroy W. Foote collection.

then he became suddenly and stubbornly silent and spoke in his broken English.

His cancer is rapidly eating away his life. The right cheek is entirely gone, including a portion of the lower lip. He would not allow Dr. Benedict to dress it or Mrs. Benedict to do anything for his comfort, save to give him the coffee and a bottle of milk.

He now seems very shaky and is evidently drawing near his end. It seems as if the Humane Society should look after him, and care for him, even if it was necessary to do so by force, or else some day he will be found a corpse in some out of the way place, the victim of a-craze, want, neglect and exposure.

Deep River New Era, Friday, February 1, 1889

THE OLD LEATHER MAN

Is now over 70 years of age. He has tramped by your doors for more than 30 years. A terrible cancer is eating his jaw away and it does not seem possible that he will pull through another winter.

Davison, the Celebrated Artist,

Has several copyrighted Photos of him. Panels at 50 cents and Cabinets at 25 cents each; post paid *to any part of the country.* Or will give 3 Panels for $1.00, or 5 Cabinets for $1.00.

A. J. DAVISON,
Colchester, Conn.

This advertisement, using the circa 1885 woodcut, ran from February through April of 1889 in The Deep River New Era.

Evening News, Saturday, February 9, 1889

Photographed
The Connecticut Humane society has issued a photograph of the singular nomad of Connecticut, the Old Leather Man. He is represented sitting in a chair, out of doors, clad in the suit that has made him famous. His countenance is by no means devoid of intelligence, but the terrible marks of the disease, which attacked him, are manifest.

Penny Press, Monday, February 11, 1889

DEEP RIVER

The Leather Man was due here Feb. 10th. Many doubt if they will ever see him after this trip.

Penny Press, Saturday, February 16, 1889

PERSONALS

By the telephone, a message kindly sent by Mrs. Guy, of Middlefield, we learn that the Old Leather Man passed her house this morning and that his condition appeared deplorable.

Wandering on His Way

THE LEATHER MAN LOOKS
CAREWORN AND MISERABLE

The old leather man made his appearance in Staddle Hill this morning, just six days late. He was looking about as tough as any ordinary mortal could and informed those with whom he came in contact that last night he slept in the woods. He visited the residence of Mr. Fisher, as usual, and there obtained a hot bowl of coffee. The cancer on his lip now covers one side of his face, and a large cavity in his neck, the result of the awful disease, shows itself. The old fellow was mum from the word go and refused to say any thing except what was necessary. After obtaining what he desired he made his departure up the road and probably by this time is safely housed in one of his caves below the town. A telephonic message recorded in another item shows that he had passed Mrs. Guy's in Middlefield.

The Old Leather Man, photographer and location unknown. Note the bandaged finger on his right hand.
Courtesy of the Plymouth Historical Society.

Bristol Herald, Thursday, February 21, 1889

The Old Leather Man

A BRIEF OUTLINE OF HIS LIFE AND CUSTOMS

The deplorable condition of the Old Leather Man, who as nearly every one in this vicinity already knows, is suffering from a cancer which is slowly but surely eating his life away, renders him a fit subject for comment at this time. There has been considerable said in the papers from time to time about this depraved and certainly mysterious individual, still there are comparatively few of our readers who have really seen him.

From The Deep River New Era, *April 1889 advertisement, enlargement of the circa 1885 woodcut of the Old Leather Man.*

THE OLD LEATHER MAN

For the benefit of those, we produce an illustration of the old man in today's HERALD. It will be noticed that he is sitting down enjoying a repast, probably furnished him by some kindhearted friend along this route. If the whole picture of the place where he was seated when the photographer exposed the lenses of his camera from his secret hiding place was pictured out, it would show him as being seated on the lower step of a grocery store in one of the country towns in the south-ern part of the state. It will also be noticed that his leather haversack is close beside him.

The likeness of this historical old chap is a good one that is as he looked before the cancer had made such great inroads on his countenance. Now his lower lip is nearly gone, his face is swollen and a careworn and discouraged expression in his eye. His gait is unsteady and he trudges along as though painfully apparent that the end is not far distant, but he does not falter in his endless rounds of travel. Day after day, in sunshine or storm, summer or winter, finds him trudging along over the same endless route. It is estimated that he is between 60 and 70 years of age and that he has been tramping from place to place, sleeping in poorly constructed huts in the woods and living upon food given him by kindly disposed persons along his line of march for more than 20 years. Never was he known to steal or beg. When at his huts, which he has built himself of branches of trees, rails and stones, he never burns anything but the dead wood lying about on the ground. The HERALD man can distinctly remember visiting one of his huts near Forestville two years ago yesterday. It was indeed a dilapidated looking shelter for a human being to stay in over night and call it "home." This hut was afterwards disturbed by boys and he abandoned it and now makes no stop after passing through Forestville until he reaches Queen Street, between Plainville and Southington, where he takes to the East Mountain near the Morroways' place. His course lies through Berlin, Middletown, to the Connecticut River, which he follows nearly to the sound, thence easterly to Stamford and around to Danbury, Watertown, and Reynolds Bridge, making the circuit through Polkville Street to Forestville. His regular time to arrive at any one place is every 34 days, but since the blizzard of last March he has not appeared so regularly. During his last trip he was four days behind his regular scheduled time. Mr. Isaac Beach's residence in Forestville has always been a place where the Leather Man has found a hearty welcome and a good meal awaiting him. Mr. Beach and his family have used every effort to draw from him something concerning his past history, but their efforts have been in vain.

THE LEATHER MAN IN TERRYVILLE

A Terryville correspondent writes to the *Times* as follows: "Why does the Connecticut Humane Society allow this pitiable object to roam longer? He was seen on the 12th, about 4 o'clock, in the north part of Plymouth, going to his cave in the ledges. Mr. Gladwin saw him coming very slowly and watching him, saw that his lip was in a very bad condition and while in sight of his house he fell several times. On Thursday two young men living near, by my request, went in search of him, thinking that he might still be in the woods. Following his tracks, which went in a different way than usual and which showed several places where he had fallen from exhaustion, when they reached his cave they found that he had gone. Nearby was a small tree which he had tried to cut down with his hatchet and had failed. In the cave was some wood which he had left on some former trip and also a piece of wood that looked as if he had used it in eating boiled meat and there were some old leather shoes. His cave is a shelving rock, open only at the north and south ends, which he has closed by some brush and some boards left in the woods by a picnic party several years ago. After this the young men followed his tracks to the road leading from Burlington to Bristol and seeing that he was out of danger of freezing in the woods, they returned to his cave and built a fire. In a very short time it was quite warm. There is not as much danger of his freezing after he gets to any of his caves as there is on the way in trying to get there."

The *Times* says editorially that it is not the duty of the Connecticut Humane Society to look after this determined vagabond, so much as it is the duty of the selectmen of the particular town where he may chance to be stopping. He has once or twice been arrested and lodged in comfortable quarters for mere humanity's sake, as his recent assignment to the Hartford Hospital, but he will not stay in any civilized situation, he breaks away and tramps off for the woods and ledges, be these far or near. He is a wretched object, quite old and suffering from a frightful cancer on the lip. Death will be his only release and it is probably not far off.

Penny Press, Thursday, February 21, 1889
CLINTON

The old Leather Man passed through here on his regular route bound west, on time exactly. He stopped at Ebens' as usual and got his coffee and 3 cigars, one more than he generally gets (as Eben says, "One more for luck"). The following dates are correct for the last year and a half. 1887. July 1, Aug. 16, Sept. 22, Oct. 27, Dec. 1, 1888. Jan. 6, Feb. 12, March 22, April 27, June 1,

July 9, Aug. 16, Sept. 23, Oct. 30, Dec. 6, 1889. Jan. 13, Feb. 20.

The cancerous formation has eaten the side of his face and neck.

Deep River New Era, Friday, February 22, 1889
HIGGANUM

The old leather man passed through here Sunday, seven days behind. He walks somewhat slower than he has been in the habit of doing. Possibly this may be his last, as he is failing very fast. His life's journey is nearly completed.

Deep River New Era, Friday, February 22, 1889
DEEP RIVER

Mr. Louis Bourglay, more familiarly known as the old Leather Man, passed through here on his usual route last Tuesday, evidently to the surprise of many, who thought he would have succumbed before now to the cancerous wounds on his face. The old man intends to die game.

Deep River New Era, Friday, February 22, 1889
CENTERBROOK

The old Leatherman passed through this place Tuesday morning. He eagerly accepted the food given him, and then continued his journey.

Deep River New Era, Friday, February 22, 1889

The Old Leather Man Makes One More Trip
He came into Chester Feb. 18th, Monday, at about 2 o'clock p.m.

I met him in the street and got out of my carriage in the rain and stopped him and asked him in French, to let me examine his face. He replied in French, "Oui," that is yes.

I found that his lower lip was cut down to the chin bone and there is a hole under the tongue coming through on the left side of the windpipe to the outside of the throat about the size of an egg. Through this

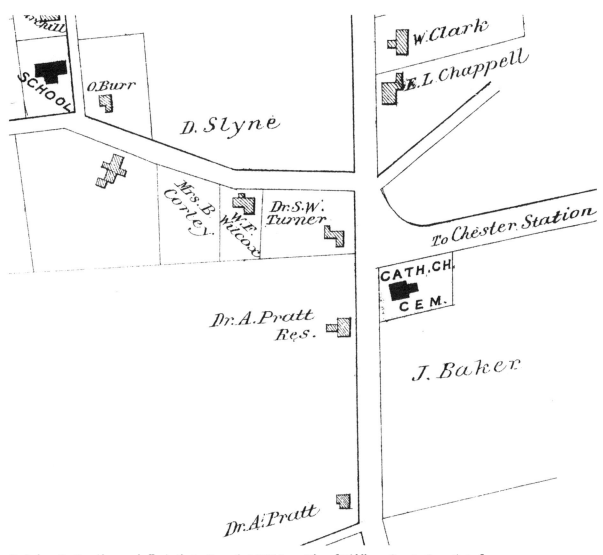

Dr. Ambrose Pratt's residences and office in Chester, Connecticut. F. W. Beers, Atlas of Middlesex County, Connecticut, 1874.

hole the spittle and matter ran down upon some old rags that hung over his breast.

He has a cancer of the lip and it has eaten down through to the outside of the throat as described. He seemed to breathe short and acted weak.

I don't think he will make many more trips, but find himself unable to walk some morning on waking up and if not found, will starve and die and then let him rest in peace and who will mourn?

Dr. Pratt

Brewster Standard,
Friday evening, February 22, 1889

The old "Leather Man" passed through the town of Southeast on his way to Connecticut on the 6th inst.

His appearance at Sodom is very regular, varying from thirty to thirty-five days, and his course is always the same. He comes from the town of North Salem to Southeast, but his exact route is not known.

He is usually seen early in the morning in the vicinity of Brush Hollow and it is thought that he spends the night on Joe's Hill. At the residence of Miss Kate Crane, in the Southeast Center, he usually arrives at ten o'clock, and after obtaining food proceeds on his journey. His route is north, thence east across the country to DeForest Corners, and thence northeast to the vicinity of Ball's Pond. At a recent visit, while the old man was eating his lunch at Miss Crane's, Walter McCulloh, superintendent of construction at Sodom Dam, succeeded in obtaining an excellent photograph of him, showing quite clearly the cancer on the left side of the old man's mouth and cheek. Since the in-

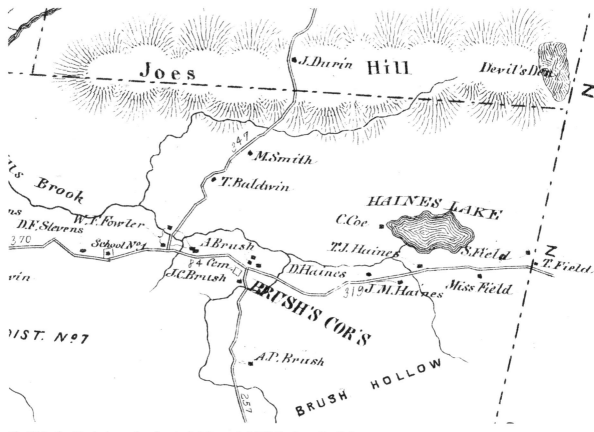

The Old Leather Man had a number of cave/rock shelters on Joe's Hill, Southeast, New York.
F. W. Beers, Ellis, and Soule, Atlas of New York and Vicinity, 1867.

formation and development of the cancer the old man has added to his costume a scarf of rags, with which he frequently wipes and sometimes hides from view his ghastly face.

Meriden Daily Journal, Thursday, March 14, 1889

Fairfield, Conn., March 14. The "Old Leather Man" passed through here yesterday. He appeared very weak, but positively refused assistance.

Stamford Weekly Advocate, Friday, March 22, 1889
LONG RIDGE

The old "leather man" passed through The Farms a few days ago. It was his first trip in twenty years in that neighborhood. He presents a distressing spectacle.

The Old Leather Man, photographer and location unknown.
Leroy W. Foote collection.

New York Times, Monday, March 25, 1889

The Old "Leather Man" Dead

The queer old hermit who has been known throughout this state for some years as the "Leather Man" from his unique apparel, which was made of skins, was found dead in his cave on the George Dell Farm in Mount Pleasant, near Sing Sing, yesterday. His head was badly bruised, whether accidentally or intentionally is not known. He was about 60 years old and a Frenchman by birth, but no one was ever able to find out his name. He was a harmless old man and the people of the region in which he located himself were generally willing to give him the little food he needed. Coroner Sutton will hold an inquest in the case tomorrow afternoon, in Sing Sing, at 2 o'clock.

Sing-Sing (Ossining), New York, to the Hartford Times
Western Union Telegraph
Monday, March 25, 1889

"Old Leather Mans" lower jaw eaten away by cancer supposed to be cause of death inquest 2 o'clock today will hold body if desired answer.

Geo H. Sutton Coroner

Hartford Times, Monday evening, March 25, 1889

"The Old Leather Man" Gone

FOUND DEAD IN A CAVE

A GREAT SUFFERER FROM CANCER
True Story of His Life

STRANGE HISTORY OF A FRENCHMAN WHO BECAME CRAZY AND FOR TWENTY-FIVE YEARS WAS A WANDERER TO ATONE FOR A DISASTROUS FAILURE IN EARLY LIFE.

The queer old hermit who has been known throughout this state for some years as the "Leather Man," from his unique apparel, which was made of skins, was found dead in his cave on the George Dell farm in Mount Pleasant, near Sing Sing, N.Y., on Sunday. His head was badly bruised, whether accidentally or intentionally is not known.

The cave/rock shelter where the Old Leather Man died, on George Dell's farm in Mount Pleasant, New York. Leroy W. Foote collection.

Last fall a cancer developed on the left side of his lower lip and it had eaten away a greater part of the lip and made a hole through the jaw into the throat. His pitiable condition led last December to his arrest, on Staddle Hill, near Middletown, by Chief-of-Police Chapman, at the instigation of R. L. De Zeng, agent for the Connecticut Humane Society. The "Old Leather Man," when arrested, was eating near Fisher's gristmill, one of the few places where he made periodical stops on his tour about the State. The old man was brought to the Hartford Hospital. He arrived here on December 3, in the afternoon, having been brought from Middletown in a team by Agents Thrall and De Zeng. All efforts to detain him were fruitless and after remaining here about an hour he took his little leather bag and resumed his journey, for the officers of the hospital had no power to detain him. An attempt was made to induce him to change his leather garments for some of cloth, but he objected. On the following Sunday, December 9, he appeared at the house of Mr. J. F. Barnard, in North Haven. It was cold and wet. The old man was dripping with rain and mud.

No one had ever known of his knocking at a door before. He was brought to the fire by the family, and they were given a chance that few have had to a close inspection of this curious character. He was a pitiable object, cold and wet, half of his lower lip on his left side eaten away, and under the left side of his jaw was a bunch as large as a large orange, very red, but not a sore. He

Ossining, New York. The Old Leather Man had at least two cave/rock shelters on the farm of George Dell (right center) and at least one on the Ryder farm (left) in Mount Pleasant, New York. F. W. Beers, Ellis, and Soule, Atlas of New York and Vicinity, 1867.

THE WESTERN UNION TELEGRAPH COMPANY.

This Company TRANSMITS and DELIVERS messages only on conditions limiting its liability, which have been assented to by the sender of the following message. Errors can be guarded against only by repeating a message back to the sending station for comparison, and the company will not hold itself liable for errors or delays in transmission or delivery of **Unrepeated Messages**, beyond the amount of tolls paid thereon, nor in any case where the claim is not presented in writing within sixty days after sending the message.
This is an **UNREPEATED MESSAGE**, and is delivered by request of the sender, under the conditions named above.

THOS. T. ECKERT, General Manager.   NORVIN GREEN, President.

NUMBER	SENT BY	REC'D BY	CHECK
116	B2	a	H Collect Day

WESTERN UNION TEL. CO. MAR 25 1889 HARTFORD, CT. 88

Received at _____ 11.57

Dated Sing Sing ny 25
To Hartford Times
"Old Leather mans" lower jaw
eaten away by cancer supposed
to be cause of death
inquest 2 o'clock today will
hold body if desired answer.
                Geo H Sutton Coroner

Coroner's telegraph about the Old Leather Man. Courtesy of the Middlesex County Historical Society.

Woodcut of the Old Leather Man by an unknown artist, circa 1889.

pointed to his lip when offered an apple, and shook his head. No doubt he had been nearly starved, because he was unable to eat the food given him. He was given plenty of hot coffee and milk, bread, cake and pie, by the family. He seemed nearly famished. He could only eat food by crumbling it into the coffee, of which he drank six large bowlfuls of the softened food. He had a large leather bag, which was very heavy. It contained as far as could be seen old bootlegs and an axe. He had a cloth bag also, which seemed full. While eating, he had a piece of leather, which he put over his sore lip to keep the food from it. His clothes were a work of art, and should be preserved. They were made of pieces of leather sewn together with thongs, like belt lacing. His trousers were of the same material. His coat was very heavy and long, and had numerous pockets on the inside, as could be seen by the leather stitches on the outside. His boots had wooden soles, two or three inches thick. His hat was entirely made of leather. It was made like a soldier's cap with a visor, all seamed up the same as his clothes. He had a woolen shirt on. His forehead, when he took off his cap to shake it, was high and white; his hair brown, fine and curly, although matted, and showing few gray hairs; his eyes large and dark blue. He had a wandering, innocent and at the same time intelligent look. He seemed grateful and furtively watched every move as if afraid of something. He had a piece of coarse cloth on which he wiped his lip. When given a piece of soft linen and told to take it, he intently examined it, looked curiously at a small hole and shook his head. He was offered tobacco, pipe and matches, all of which he declined with a shake of the head. When he was warm and had eaten enough, he got up to go. He was told to sit and warm himself as long as he liked. He simply pointed up the road, and with an expressive gesture indicated that he must go.

The old fellow had been failing rapidly since his exposure in the blizzard of last March, but his wandering, restless spirit was never curbed, and up to the day of his death he continued the lonely circuitous tour of wandering in Connecticut and eastern New York, which he has followed for the past twenty-five years by night and by day. When he began his pilgrimages about Connecticut, people were afraid of him. Women living in the country, if they chanced to see him coming, locked the outside doors of their home, and screened by curtains, would peek out and watch him pass along the roads. After a year or two they got used to him, and fear gave place to curiosity. During all the years of his wandering about the state he had never been known to utter a word or sentence, which could be understood by his hearers. His name was given him years ago. The peculiar garments of leather, which he wore, are the same as those worn by him when he appeared twenty-five years ago. They have become worn from time to time and patched until at present there is little left of the original leather.

From documents, which he lost some years ago, but which were found by others, his life's story was discovered for the first time. It is stranger than fiction, a tragic, mournful romance. Crazy Jules Bourglay, "the old leather man," was a broken-hearted, shattered-brained creature that did silent and systematic penance for his disastrous failure in early life. It has been learned from authentic sources that "the old leather man" is of French parentage and was born in France in the said old town of Lyons about 65 years ago. His father was a wood dealer, who gave him a liberal education. Young Bourglay became acquainted with a beautiful and accomplished daughter of a wealthy leather merchant named Laron. They fell in love with each other and became engaged before the parents were aware of the attachment. Mr. Laron was greatly incensed when he learned of the affair, but young Bourglay argued his case in so able and manly a manner as to soften the rich man's heart, and he finally decided to make an offer to Jules. This was to take him into the leather business for a year, and if he proved himself energetic and possessed of good business qualities, he was to have as a reward the hand of the daughter in marriage. On the other hand, if he proved unworthy of confidence, he must give up his suit and go away from Paris.

Jules accepted, of course, and was soon in the office of his prospective father-in-law, as a confidential man and agent. This was in 1857 the year when leather fell 40 per cent. Bourglay had no inkling of this unforeseen danger, and thinking he saw an opportunity to contribute toward filling his employer's coffers, he speculated largely with a commodity that was eventually to drag him down to ruin and disgrace. Finally the crash came. Thousands of men in the leather trade were either ruined or thrown out of work, and as poor Jules reeled away from the office with the curses of his impoverished employer ringing in his ears, his mind became turned. He was found two days later wandering about the street in a half-crazed condition, calling on his loved ones with endearing names and cursing the ill luck that had thwarted his hopes of a bright future. His father took him home, and he was tenderly nursed, but to no purpose. He became a raving maniac. For two years he was confined in a madhouse. From there he finally escaped to this country, where all trace of him was lost for years. His relatives finally obtained information of his whereabouts, and wrote to the New York authorities giving his past history, and directing them to spare no expense in finding out his condition, both mentally and physically. He was discovered traveling through Litchfield County, this state, as a plumber, noted for eccentric behavior, and clad entirely in sole leather. He never took anything but food or tobacco for his work and he always slept in barns. He was very reticent about this past history, and would only give his name. When asked if he wished to return to France he quickly replied, "no, no," with a shudder of fear. His relatives were informed that he was harmless and abhorred the society of men or the idea of returning to France. Since then nothing has been heard from them, and he has been wandering about the country in his heavy suit of leather, doing penance, as is supposed, for his disastrous failure in life. He forsook the plumbing business years ago.

His age may be anywhere from 60 to 70 years.

The picture, which we give of the old fellow, is from a photograph taken last October, for which he himself consented to sit. The cancer at that time was quite noticeable and can be seen in the picture on the left lip.

Waterbury Daily American, Monday, March 25, 1889

His Dead Body Reported Found in the Woods

THE FATE SO LONG FEARED FOR HIM HAS
PROBABLY OVERTAKEN HIM, THOUGH
PARTICULARS ARE WANTING—THE
MYSTERY SURROUNDING HIM.

Hartford, March 25.—Information received in this city from Mt Pleasant, N.Y., announces the finding of the body of a man in the woods near Sing Sing Sunday, which according to description given is undoubtedly that of the old Leather man, a character well known throughout this state, who tramped from town to town continually, subsisting on charity but always refusing shelter. It will surprise no one if the above information proves absolutely correct. It is the end that has been expected by all who have known of the rapid advance of the cancer on his under lip.

The story of this strange character is well known from the many, many descriptions that have been published of him in all papers. The cancer was caused by exposure to weather, his face having been frozen several times in his wandering from town to town, never accepting shelter, and from smoking the butts of cigars which he picked up.

Numerous "histories" of the man have been published, but an *American Representative* has traced each to newspaper fiction. He certainly was a Frenchman and the most common story was that he escaped from an asylum in France where he was confined after being crossed in love and after having lost his property in the leather failure in 1857. But this story originated with an account published in these columns some years ago and signed by a name which afterward proved to belong to no one in the town whence the story came. No previous story had born such marks of genuineness.

As pointed out here many times, the most remarkable thing about it all is that people 75 years old tell about just such a man traveling periodically on this same course—from eastern New York into central and southern Connecticut and back again—when they were children. Now, this man did not appear to be over 50 years old at the most, allowing everything for wonderful preservation through pedestrianism.

According to the records kept of his regular appearance once in 30 days in towns in this vicinity, he would just about have arrived near Sing Sing last week.

We may now expect a revival of some of the fictitious stories. As he never said half a dozen words to anybody, they cannot have come from him.

Inquest of Coroner, George H. Sutton
Sing Sing, New York, March 24th and 25th, 1889

Extracts from the testimony of witness

JURORS ON THE INQUEST
John M. Terwilliger, Charles Ryder, Richard Austin, Eugene Hall, Ezra Bouton, Simeon C. Washburn, John L. Birdsall

WITNESS ON THE INQUEST
Joel D. Madden, M. D., & Charles S. Collins, M.D, Testified as to Cause of Death: The immediate cause of his death is blood poisoning. It resulted from lupus, or "wolf" cancer, which had made frightful ravages in his mouth, almost destroying the lower jaw and so affected the throat that for a long time before his death ensued it must have been impossible to swallow anything but liquids, so that at last starvation was probably added to his other pangs. He most likely has been dead for at least three or four days when he was found.

Henry Miller, carpenter, Town of Mt. Pleasant, testified as to finding the body on the farm of George Dell: I went out for a walk with my wife on Sunday morning last, my wife expressed a wish to see the retreat of the Leather Man, so, we went there. As we were entering the hut, we thought the man was asleep, but at second glance saw that he was dead. His hair and beard was mottled with blood, his face swollen and distorted.

George Dell, farmer, testified: He frequently stopped on my farm for a little over five years last past, in a rude structure he made in the woods for a shanty or a hut. I had a conversation with him once. I could not hold him long in conversation. I thought he was a Frenchman. I asked him a few words in French and he answered promptly in French. This man frequented the place where he was found dead often. He never came to my home to beg, nor did I ever give him any food. I never saw him under the influence of drink of any kind. He never asked my permission to build the hut on my land, and I didn't object. I have seen him in the hut a number of times, but could not talk with him. On a cold or stormy day I would say to him, "why don't you build a fire?" He would answer, "a good fire, a good fire." I never saw him cooking anything. When I first saw him, twenty-eight years ago, he wore then the same suit or one similar to it, and made of small pieces of leather, mostly boot legs sewed together with leather bands. Two books each made of leaves of brown paper, full of figures were found; but I don't think he could read or write.

Reuben Whitson, farmer, testified: I have known the Leather Man for over twenty-eight years past. The last twenty years I saw him once in every two months pass my house, and he never varied his line of march. He carried a large leather bag made of bootlegs. I do not know how he lived, as he never begged, nor his name, nor any of his relatives.

Walter L. Whitson, farmer, testified: I have known the Leather Man ever since I was a small boy. I often tried to get him into conversation, but he would never reply. I offered him a chew of tobacco, but he did not answer me. The last time I saw him he looked ill and did not have the large bag. He was a mystery to me. I never knew him to work anywhere. He was about sixty years old.[2]

Death Record
Mount Pleasant, New York

(See page 113.)

Meriden Daily Journal, Tuesday March 26, 1889

A Fugitive From Justice
ANOTHER VERSION OF THE OLD
MAN'S MYSTERIOUS EARLY LIFE
Terryville, March 26.—John Welton, well known throughout the north-western part of the state as an authority on matters of local history, says the Old Leather Man, who was found dead, near Mount Pleasant, N.Y., was no lovesick Frenchman, but that he was

2. Stewart, 1889.

a fugitive from justice and a Negro. "Years ago," says Mr. Welton, who is a resident of this village, "there was a notorious resort not far from New Hartford known as the Barkhamsted lighthouse. It was a rickety log cabin situated on a high hill and heated by a fire in a huge fireplace. The light shining through the crevices and windows could be seen for many a mile and that is how it derived its name. The lighthouse was the rendezvous for a gang of thieves, white men and colored, who committed crimes of all kinds. After a series of particularly bold depredations, the gang was broken up and the authorities were very anxious to capture some of the band. This 'Old Leather Man,' who appeared in public not long after, was one of the half-breed Negroes born and brought up in the place. He chose the disguise of leather to conceal his identity and liked it so well that he continued to wear it until his death. He was of Negro descent rather than of Caucasian. I have watched his movements for years and think I am certain in his history. He didn't steal, that is, after he become so notorious. He didn't have to. Sympathetic women and curious men gave him a better living than he could steal; and as to his suffering from out door life, he was as happy as an Indian before stoves were invented." His name, according to himself, was Jules Bourglay. Most of the so-called caves in which he slept are well known and have been often visited. Where his stopping places were disturbed he invariably abandoned them. Not far from here was his most comfortable resting place. It is a natural cave, being part of a "Tory den" made famous in the Revolutionary war by Tories who found it convenient to hide from the world. Bourglay's body is now in Sing Sing, awaiting the inquest of Coroner Sutton which was postponed to this afternoon. The bruises which were first reported upon him proved upon investigation to be nothing but the effects of the cancer which has for some time troubled him and which was indirectly the probable cause of his death. The body will be buried by the Sing Sing authorities.

New York Times, Tuesday, March 26, 1889

His Life of Penance
THE STRANGE STORY OF THE FAMOUS
VAGRANT, THE LEATHER MAN
The Leather Man, found dead in a cave near Sing Sing on Sunday, had tramped for nearly 40 years over the

CERTIFIED TRANSCRIPT OF DEATH
STATE OF NEW YORK
DEPARTMENT OF HEALTH

NAME: Known by the Leatherman

SEX: Male

DATE OF DEATH: March 20, 1889

DISTRICT NO.:

PLACE OF DEATH: (Street & No.) Mt. Pleasant

INDEX NO.:

DATE OF BIRTH: Unknown

AGE: 50

PLACE OF BIRTH: Unknown

SERVED IN US ARMED FORCES (Years)

MARITAL STATUS:

OCCUPATION: Unknown

FATHER'S NAME: Unknown

MOTHER'S MAIDEN NAME: Unknown

CERTIFYING PHYSICIAN OR CORONER: George W. Sutton, Coroner

MANNER OF DEATH: Blood Poisoning Resulting from Cancer

FUNERAL HOME:

PLACE OF BURIAL: Sparta Cemetary

DATE FILED:

This is to certify that the information concerning the death of the above named person is a true and accurate transcription of the information recorded on the original local certificate of death on file with the local registrar of <u>Mt. Pleasant</u>, New York.
Name of Locality

GENEALOGY PURPOSES ONLY

_____
Signature of Local Registrar

DATE May 21, 2004

Do not accept this transcript unless the raised seal of the issuing locality is affixed thereon.
Any Alteration Invalidates This Certificate
See Reverse Side For A List of Security Features Used In This Form

DOH-4144 (7/2000)

VALID DOCUMENT CONTAINS STATE SEAL IN FLUORESCENT INK ON BACK - VIEW AT ANGLE

Death certificate for the Old Leather Man. State of New York, Department of Health, VR Mount Pleasant, New York.

country roads in Westchester county, in this State, and in New Haven, Fairfield, and Litchfield Counties in Connecticut. His suit of clothes, patched and re-patched with leather, made him a unique figure among tramps and gave him his name. Caves scattered about the country he frequented were his chosen abiding places, and when remote from these he readily found shelter in the barns of the farmers, who never feared that he would do their property injury. Farmers' wives willingly fed him, and vainly tried to get him to talk. Country school children gave him pennies and sweetmeats, and no one seemed to fear him. The long staff he carried was never used, save as an aid to locomotion.

Thousands of Connecticut-born boys and girls have gazed after the strange figure and wondered what he carried in the huge leather sack that was always slung across his shoulder. Two years ago, when the old fellow was found lying ill in a cave near Woodbury, Conn., the secrets of the old sack were discovered by the young men who found and nursed him back to life. They were a French prayer book printed in 1844, a pipe of his own make, a hatchet, a small tin pail, a small spider,[3] a jackknife, and an awl, the lot constituting his library and housekeeping utensils. Suspended about his neck was a crucifix and the usual scapular worn by Catholics. His only underclothing was a knit woolen jacket.

He could rarely be induced to speak to any one, but when he did speak it was in the patois of Southern France, of which he was a native. A romance there certainly was in his life, for he was free to confess that his method of life was a penance. Something less than a decade ago an emissary from his relatives in France overtook the old man on his tramp near Wilton, Conn., and tried to induce him to return to his native country. This agent refused to reveal the old man's personality, saying only that his people in France were very wealthy and well born. Partly from words dropped by the Leather Man to a Professor at Yale College, who once got him to talk, and partly from an old Frenchman in Bridgeport who claimed to know his relatives, this story of his life was formulated and has been commonly accepted:

While a young man he fell in love with a girl employed in a leather manufactory near Marseilles, owned by his father. The father opposed the match; the girl rejected the proposals of a dishonorable alliance with

Entrance to Sparta Cemetery on Revolutionary Road, Ossining, New York. Photo by D.W. DeLuca, 2000.

the son made by the parent; the girl disappeared. The young man became convinced there had been foul play, and eventually that the girl had been murdered through the machination of his parents. He then left home and his country, and never let his friends hear from him. Frequent publications in American papers of the man and his wanderings, which were always scheduled so that he appeared at certain places at regularly recurring periods, brought the attention of his brothers to him. His identity was absolutely established. But the Leather Man refused to quit the vagrant life he followed persistently as a sort of expiation for the crime he believed his father had either personally committed or had hired some one to commit.

Coroner Sutton held an inquest at Sing Sing yesterday and heard how Henry Miller, an employee on the aqueduct, had on Sunday taken his wife to see the cave on George Dell's farm and had discovered the old man's body under the shelving rock which served him as a shelter. Mr. Dell and Reuben and Walter Whitson testified that they had known the Leather Man for 30 years. The Whitsons last seen him two weeks ago. He was then very ill and hardly able to walk, but he declined to accept assistance. Drs. Madden and Collins testified that death was due to blood poisoning resulting from a cancer, which had eaten away part of the lower jaw. The verdict of the Corner's jury was:

"That the Leather Man came to his death from cancer and inability to obtain or take food."

The body was buried[4] yesterday afternoon in the

3. A *spider* was a cast-iron frying pan with attached legs for setting on coals.

4. Before burial his remains had been removed to the White Dorsey undertaking rooms, where many curious visitors viewed them. Nearby was the leather suit that gave him his name.

Sparta Cemetery. The Coroner has two books,[5] which were found in the cave, made of brown paper and full of figures and hieroglyphics, which could not be deciphered.

Hartford Times, Wednesday, March 27, 1889

The Mystery of the "Old Leather Man"

[From the Waterbury American]

He certainly was a Frenchman and the most common story was that he escaped from an asylum in France where he was confined after being crossed in love and after having lost his property in the leather failure in 1857. But this story originated with an account published in these columns some years ago and signed by a name which afterward proved to belong to no one in the town whence the story came. No previous story had born such marks of genuineness.

As pointed out herein many times, the most remarkable thing about it all is that people 75 years old tell about just such a man traveling periodically on this same course—from eastern New York into central and southern Connecticut—when they were children. Now, this man did not appear to be over 50 years old at the most, allowing everything for wonderful preservation through pedestrianism. According to the records kept of his regular appearance once in thirty days in towns in this vicinity, he would just about have arrived at Sing Sing last week. We may now expect a revival of some of the fictitious stories. As he never said half a dozen words to anybody, they cannot have come from him.

> To the Editor of The Times.
>
> I hate to spoil a good story, especially after I have perpetrated it myself, but I feel compelled to do so in this case. Some three years ago, one whom I considered a reliable correspondent furnished me with an apparently authentic account of the life of the Leather Man and I published it in the American. It was widely copied and ever since has appeared periodically, changed now and then by some writer, but the main facts being preserved. It is the story which you published in the best of faith last night as the "true story." Some time after the publication by me, I learned beyond peradventure that my correspon-

dent knew nothing about the matter, and that all the supposed facts were fictions. The denial, which I published, did not overtake the story, but now the general publication of it makes it incumbent upon me, in justice to the public, to again put it forth.

> C. W. Burpee.[6]
> Waterbury, Conn., March 26, 1889.

Waterbury Daily Republican, Wednesday, March 27, 1889

The Old Leather Man

The death of the Old Leather Man removes a unique and mysterious figure. He was, in respect of raiment at least, the embodiment of the imaginary personage sung by Mother Goose in her ditty:

> "One misty, moisty morning, when cloudy was the
>   weather,
> I chanced to meet an old man clothed all in
>   leather."

But there was this marked difference between the character depicted in the anserine prophecy and its modern fulfillment: According to the nursery-loving mother-in-law of THOMAS FLEET, the marvelously clad hero of her rhyme;

> ". . . began to compliment and I began to grin;
> How do you do and how do you do and how do you
>   do again;"

While the taciturn Old Leather Man who has just passed away was never known to compliment, or indulge in any other conversation.

Who this strange being was nobody knew. Various stories have been invented about him:

Some say he was a Frenchmen named JULES BOURGLAY;

Others that he was a mulatto;

But it is all guesswork. His history is unknown.

Was he a misanthrope whose heart had been shriveled by some bitter experience, which made him hate and shun his fellow man?

Was he a criminal restlessly driven about, like a Wandering Jew, by fear, remorse and biting of conscience?

---

5. Could the papers in the books be the same ones the Old Leather Man showed James F. Rodgers in 1885? Could those curious characters represent the Old Leather Man's route?

6. Charles Winslow Burpee was editor of the Waterbury Daily American.

Was he voluntarily doing awful penance for some heinous sin?

Had he been crossed in love or worldly ambition and sought refuge in solitude from the disappointments and selfish rivalries of life?

Was there within him some strong, active mind, which by a masterly self-will he kept so securely impersonal that no evidence of its existence came to the surface; or was he only a poor, witless fool?

What a subject for a fantastic imagination!

What a nucleus for fascinating fiction!

Waterbury Daily Republican, Thursday, March 28, 1889

COMMUNICATIONS

[*The Republican* disclaims responsibility for views expressed by writers of communications published in this department.]

The Old Leather Man in Waterbury

To the Editor of the Republican:

The various comments in the papers upon the death of the Old Leather Man recall very vividly his regular appearance on our streets twenty-five years ago. In those days one of his regular stopping places was at the house of Deacon Aaron Benedict on South Main Street, where he invariably appeared in time for a good breakfast, which was always accompanied by his favorite beverage, coffee.

Occasionally as he passed the company office just before, we would call him in and seek to draw him out. "What did you have for breakfast?" "Good coffee." "Where did you sleep last night?" "On the street." All efforts beyond this were fruitless. So uniform had been his replies that we were accustomed to say as he passed: "There goes Good Coffee."

In later years he seems to have avoided the larger towns, while continuing the same tramp life over a little different route. He was always very civil and harmless; so far as could be judged by his appearance in this region. I do not think he had any Negro blood in his veins as some have stated and I judge that he must have been much more than fifty years old, as he seemed at least that, many years ago.

E. L. BRONSON

Waterbury, March 27, 1889.

Bristol Weekly Press, Thursday, March 28, 1889

The Old Leather Man

FOUND DEAD IN A CAVE

When the old leather man's body was found there was no trace of the leather bag he used to carry. His coat weighed 20 pounds.

FORESTVILLE

Chauncey Hotchkiss, who has taken a great interest in the old leather man, whose death is noted elsewhere, has in his possession many letters received in correspondence with persons familiar with the old man's habits along his route.

Meriden Daily Journal, Friday, March 29, 1889

The Old Leather Man

NO TRUTH IN THE SUPPOSED

TRUE STORIES OF HIS LIFE

C. W. Burpee of Waterbury American, in which paper the first story of the Old Leather Man appeared some years ago, says that he has learned beyond peradventure that the writer of the yarn knew nothing about the matter and that all the supposed facts were fictions. This is borne out by A. D. Eastwood of Bristol, who says that the statement in the old man's history that he was in France in 1857 is incorrect, as he distinctly remembers that Jules Bourglay was on his wanderings through Stepney in 1856 and was not then wholly clad in leather, but wore only a leather cap, patches of leather on the knees and seat of his trousers, on his elbows and a patch on one shoulder where he carried his leather sack. The patches were added to year by year till his garb was entirely of leather, but he always had warm woolen underclothing.

Middlesex County Record, Friday, March 29, 1889

HIGGANUM

The "Leather Man," so called is stated as being dead and buried. Your correspondent is safe in stating that he saw the old fellow the first time he ever made this circuit through the town; when a schoolboy in Shailerville district, he passed the schoolhouse and it was quite a cu-

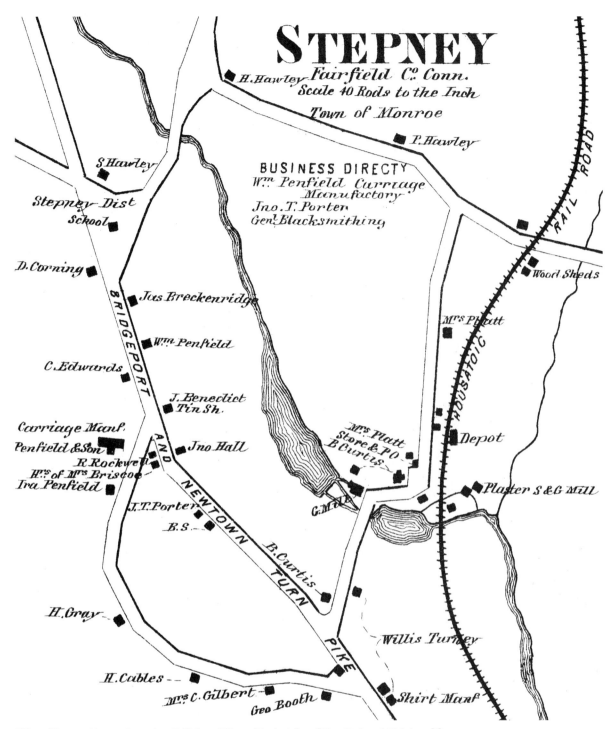

Village of Stepney, Monroe, Connecticut. F. W. Beers, Ellis, and Soule, Atlas of New York and Vicinity, 1867.

riosity to the children. His clothes looked nearly the same as the last time through. This was thirty-two or thirty-three years ago this summer. He used to make his appearance every month or six weeks and had followed that method most of the time. His passing through in cold weather was sort of an almanac for the citizens, they would say the old "Leather Man" is coming, look out for cold weather, and it was pretty sure to follow. We will leave it for a problem for you to cipher out the number of miles he has traveled.

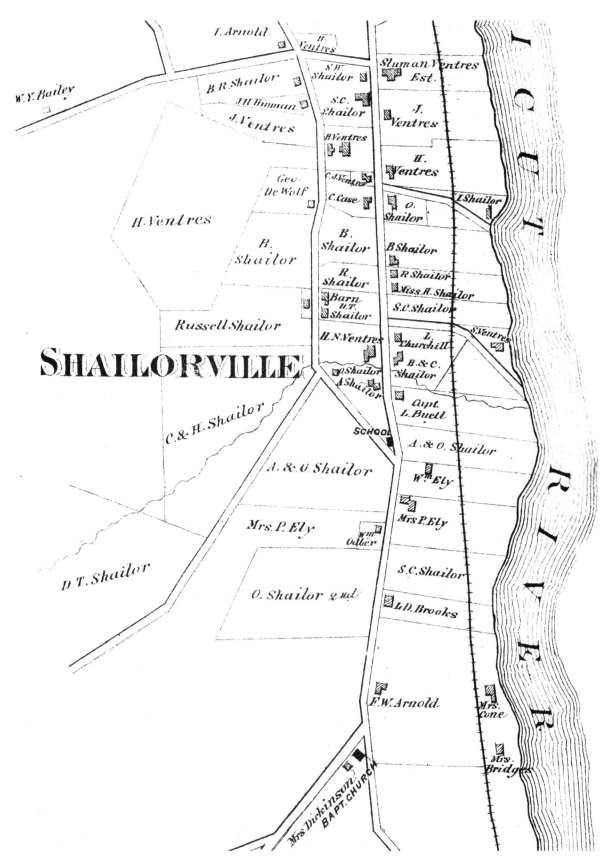

Shailorville, Haddam, Connecticut. The schoolhouse is in the lower center area of the map. F. W. Beers, Atlas of Middlesex County, Connecticut, 1874.

Cave/rock shelter near Slopers Pond, Kensington Road, Southington, Connecticut.
Photo by Eugene L. Root, 1889. Courtesy of the Meriden Historical Society.

**Meriden Daily Republican, Meriden, Connecticut,
Friday, March 29, 1889**

The Leather Man's Shoe

A. Root, an employee of the Republican Pressroom, is possessed of one of the old leather man's shoes, which that celebrity had discarded at his hut in the woods near Southington. The hut, which is made of rails placed against a rock, was discovered by Mr. Root, while gunning in the neighborhood about a year ago. Its wooden sole was partly worn out, and the leather man had evidently discarded it for a new one. It is a good souvenir in memory of the old man.

**Waterbury Daily American,
Friday, March 29, 1889**

SEYMOUR

The Leather Man's Doubles

As pointed out in the Woodbury correspondence last night, there have been various characters in the state somewhat like the Leather Man, known as "Hash," "Danbury," "Old Tim," and the like, and now one is reported who used to pass through Waterbury. He is known as "Coffee," but from personal descriptions bore no resemblance to the Leather Man. For one thing, his fingers had been frozen off at the first joint many years

ago; the Leather Man's fingers were in good condition a year ago.

A man who signs himself W. A. Sailson of Chicago, much interested in the Leather Man, says he would like to see a subscription started for a respectable burial of the old character. The latest turn to fiction about the life of the man is found in the Chicago Times. That paper says his story was drawn out of him this past winter at the time he was taken to the Middletown asylum, he fearing that death was upon him; and then follows the fiction, which has been public property for three years.

Peekskill Blade, Saturday, March 30, 1889

SHRUB OAK
CORRESPONDENCE OF THE
PEEKSKILL BLADE, MARCH 29TH, 1889

The Old Leather Man

In the Blade of March 9th, we called the attention of our readers to the fact that the "Leather man" was suffering from a cancer upon his lip, which would soon cause his death. Since that time the old fellow has been plodding along, as has always been his custom, from place to place, but his step became more feeble each day until he was at last compelled to go no farther and laid himself down to die in one of his lonely caves in the town of Mt. Pleasant about four miles northeast of Sing Sing

The Old Leather Man; woodcut by Orville F. Ireland from Shrub Oak, New York, circa 1888.

starvation was probably added to his other pangs. The physicians thought he had been dead for at least three or four days when found.

For more than 18 years he has been one of the chief objects of interest to the country folks of Westchester County and Connecticut as he has made his regular monthly trips, seldom varying an hour in his arrival at or departure from his regular stopping places. He was about five feet eight inches high and when in health would weigh about 170 pounds. His complexion was very dark either naturally or from exposure and he always wore his beard trimmed rather short. It is believed that the cancer which caused his death was produced by his face being badly frozen during the severe blizzard of March 12th, 1888. His principle cave or headquarters was in the old cave in Saw Mill woods near the south end of Stony Street and it is said that he had a vast amount of money hidden in his cave.

The "Old Leather Man" passed through Shrub Oak during the past year, going east, on the following dates:

Date	Days Out
1887	
Friday, December 16	00
1888	
Saturday, January 21	36
Monday, February 27	37
Saturday, April 7	40
Sunday, May 13	36
Monday, June 18	36
Thursday, July 26	38
Sunday, September 2	38
Thursday, October 11	39
Saturday, November 17	37
Sunday, December 23	36
1889	
Wednesday, January 30	38

village. Here he spent the last hours of his mysterious life without medical attendance, food or nursing and here his body was accidentally discovered by Henry Miller, of Mount Pleasant, who is employed on the new aqueduct. Mr. Miller went out for a walk with his wife. On Sunday morning last, they strolled to the piece of woods where the "Hut" is located, a mile from the road and a mile and a half from any other habitation. Mrs. Miller expressed a wish to see the retreat of the recluse and so they went there, when a horrible sight met their eyes. The old man lay on the ground quite dead, his livid, swollen face distorted by agony. His grizzled hair and beard were mottled with blood and his limbs showed by their contortions how fierce had been the death struggle. There were no marks of violence, however. On Monday, Coroner Sutton of Sing Sing held an inquest.

Medical testimony at the inquest revealed the immediate cause of his death to have been blood poisoning. It resulted from lupus, or "wolf" cancer, which had made frightful ravages in his mouth, almost destroying the lower jaw and so affected the throat that for a long time before his death ensued it must have been impossible to swallow anything but liquids, so that of last

The many peculiarities of the old "Leather Man" are well known to the readers of the *Blade*, a graphic description of whom was given in this paper in October 1885. He always ate his breakfast in Gilbert Darrow's grocery and dined at the residence of William E. Ireland when in this place, and he will be greatly missed by the entire community.

During the many years that he has been making his monthly trips between this place and New Haven he has never been known to hold any conversation with a human being and he died as he lived, unknown.

Democratic Register, Sing Sing, Saturday, March 30, 1889

The Suit on Exhibition

On Wednesday the old Leather Man's suit and the articles found in the cave where he died were placed on exhibition in the show window of John L. Birdsall's cigar store, next to the post-office, and all afternoon and evening big crowds stood outside looking at the leather suit which made the eccentric hermit famous, as it occupied a position as though he were in life sitting on a chair.

Meriden Daily Journal, Saturday, March 30, 1889

The Leather Man's Suit Exhibited

The leather suit worn by the "Old Leather Man," who was found dead in a cave near Sing Sing, has been placed on exhibition in a store window in Sing Sing.

The suit has been stuffed and a mask fitted to it. The figure sits on a chair. Upon the knee is the hermit's diary open, with the imitation hand resting on it.

New Britain Record, Saturday, March 30, 1889

Now that the Old Leather Man is dead, newspapers everywhere are bringing out the story of his life in various shades of romance. Some of them are very nice pretty stories too, but unfortunately they all lack probability. While it may not be that he was a criminal, it is equally unlikely that he was ever a man of educational refinement. Certainly nothing in his looks or manners betrayed acquaintances with anything but the rudest, and most barbarous style of existence.

The latest yarn that he was one of the once famous "Barkhamsted light-house" gang, and a mulatto, deserves as little credence as any other.

Connecticut Valley Advertiser, Saturday, March 30, 1889
The Old Leather Man Dead

ESSEX

The old "Leather Man's" heavy tramp is over. He was found dead in a cave in Mount Pleasant, near Sing Sing, N.Y., on Sunday last. For the past thirty years he had always stopped at Aunt Azubah Starkey's, an aged lady who lives in the South district. We trust he has gone to

John L. Birdsall's cigar store, next to the post office, Ossining, New York; postcard, early 1900s. Leroy W. Foote collection.

a better home where the wicked cease from troubling and the weary are at rest.

New York Daily News, Monday, April 1, 1889

The Leather Man's Ghost

A FRIGHTENED FARMER WHO WAS

SEARCHING THE LATE RECLUSE'S CAVE

Shrub Oak, April 1.—Since the death of the old "Leather Man" hundreds of people have visited his lonely cave in the Saw Mill Woods, near Shrub Oak, searching for money which he is supposed to have hidden away during the twenty years that he has made this spot his headquarters. On Saturday night, after Farmer Clematis Sorrell had finished his day's work, he bade his wife and daughter adieu and with his lighted torch in his hand started for the big Saw Mill Woods in quest of the late "Leather Man's" treasure.

Soon after midnight the farmer returned to his family and related a heart-rending story of his narrow escape from the clutches of the Leather Man's ghost. He said that while he was making his way out of the cave his torch was extinguished, and, having no matches, he endeavored to find his way out without a light. He was soon confronted by the Leather Man, who ignited a pile of dried sticks and beckoned for Mr. Sorrel to leave at once, which he did with all possible rapidity, running all the way home, a distance of three miles. Sorrel, who is not a drinking man, thinks the Leather Man has a double.

—New York Daily News.

Waterbury Daily Republican, Tuesday, April 2, 1889

The Old Leather Man

A WATERBURY CITIZEN WHO

ONCE CONVERSED WITH HIM

E. A. Hough of No. 5. Cossett Street once conversed with the mysterious Old Leather Man. In a conversation yesterday with a Waterbury Republican reporter he said:

"I was pretty well acquainted with the Old Leather Man, if I may so express myself. I was in the habit a number of years ago of meeting him frequently on the road. I was engaged hauling wood to Benedict & Burnham's from Reynolds Bridge and once in four weeks, almost to a day, between 8 and 11 a.m. he would appear near John Warner's, half a mile east of Reynolds Bridge. He came from Frost's bridge and then at Reynolds Bridge turning to the east and going over Plymouth Hill. There he turned towards Harwinton, passing the Episcopal Church. He always courted seclusion, kept on the back roads and in those days never entered a house, stopping merely at back doors, where he was accustomed to get something to eat. He was an inveterate tobacco chewer and passed the station at Reynolds Bridge and Curtis Hotel on Plymouth Hill, to pick up cigar stumps, which he converted into chewing tobacco. He carried a pack, made like his suit, of bootlegs.

"I notice Miss Prichard says that the man she knew had lost the tips of the fingers of one hand. The Old Leather Man's hands were perfect. He also did not look delicate, by any means. He was a short thickset man with a broad face. He never conversed with anybody when a third party was present. I held a number of conversations with him when he met me alone. He spoke English so that he could be easily understood. On one occasion I came upon him with a newspaper before him. He was seated on a bank, apparently reading it. I found it was the New York Herald and when I asked him if he could read it, he said he could. Seven or eight years ago I had quite a talk with him about a mile below Reynolds Bridge. I had given him a piece of money and that partly unloosed his tongue, particularly as he seemed to feel that I was kindly disposed toward him. He told me that he had come from France twenty-two years before, but why he came he would not say. I tried to find out what his occupation had been in France and as well as I could make out it was chopping wood. I asked him where he slept and he replied in the woods.

"Two years ago in company with my wife I passed him, but he would not talk and even seemed not to recognize me. He appeared to be in his usual health and his whiskers were neatly trimmed. Mr. Warner recently told me that he had been crossing Plymouth Hill for about twenty years. I think he was from 50 to 55 years of age. He was quiet and inoffensive and when a person came along driving a lively horse, he would get out of the way, so that his odd appearance might not frighten the horse."

Litchfield Enquirer, Thursday, April 4, 1889

GOSHEN NO. 903

We always rather liked to see the Old Leather Man in his travels from Dutchess Co., to the East and back, but lately he has traveled from Westchester Co., farther south.

HN

Meriden Daily Republican, Saturday, April 6, 1889

Photographic Exhibition

EXTRACTS FROM THE ARTICLE

The Stereopticon, Under Rev. A. H. Hall's Direction, Entertains a Large Audience. The fourth-annual exhibition of amateur photography in the Town Hall last evening was a marked success. The two views of the "Leather Man" were very well done.

Deep River New Era, Friday, April 5, 1889

PICTURES

OF THE

Old Leather Man

Davison, the Celebrated Artist,

Has several copyrighted Photos of him. Panels at 50 cents and Cabinets at 25 cents each; post paid *to any part of the country.* Or will give 3 Panels for $1.00, or 5 Cabinets for $1.00.

A. J. DAVISON,

Colchester, Conn.

Advertisement, appeared in The Deep River New Era newspaper, April 5, 1889.

Deep River New Era, Friday, April 5, 1889

The Old Leatherman[7]

The poor Leatherman is gone,
He has taken another route
He went, as he lived, all alone
No more will he travel about.

A queer and strange old hermit
Clad in garments made of leather.
He cared nothing about the fit
Or how it was put together.

"The old Leatherman passed today"
We often in the paper read.
No more will we have it to say
For the poor hermit is dead.

He has no kith or kin to mourn
Poor hermit he is now at rest.
Cheerless the life he here had bourne
We hope that now it is more blest.

And the crazy, demented mind
We hope will be made clear and bright.
And the maiden loved, he will find
In the throng to welcome his sight.

May his wrongs all there be righted
And the poor man's frame be made whole:
And his life, that here was blighted
Add happiness there to his soul.

And though no stone shall mark the spot
To tell us where they made his grave
The old man will not be forgot
In memory a place we'll save.

Chester, April 2d, 1889.

New Haven Evening Register, Monday, April 8, 1889

TIME TABLE OF THE LEATHER MAN
An Interesting Record of His Trips Kept for Six Years at the *Naugatuck Junction,*[8] S. A. Hale, *of Signal Tower No. 20,*

7. The poem is by Hattie H. Wooster of Chester, Connecticut.

8. Naugatuck Junction was the name of a railroad station in the western part of Milford. It was later changed to Devon, by which the locality is now known.

Naugatuck Junction, *Consolidated road*, furnishes the following record of the trips of the late "Old Leather Man." Mr. Hale says that the Leather Man was remarkably regular in his trips, thirty-four days being his shortest and 40 days his longest absence. In the years 1884–5 he made nineteen consecutive trips of thirty-four days each. When asked his name he always replied "Isaac." He always refused money and pointed to his left inside pocket, would say, "I got money." To most interrogations his reply was "I d'no," spoken with a rising inflection.

Record of the "Old Leather Man" as he passed Naugatuck Junction, Conn., Going West

Date	Time of day	Days Out
1883		
Friday, March 9	2:30 p.m.	—
Thursday, April 12	2:10 p.m.	34
Thursday, May 17	3:17 p.m.	35
Wednesday, June 20	2:14 p.m.	34
Wednesday, July 25	3:38 p.m.	35
Tuesday, August 28	3:05 p.m.	34
Monday, October 1	2:25 p.m.	34
Monday, November 25	2:12 p.m.	35
Monday, December 10	2:37 p.m.	35
1884		
Wednesday, January 16	10:37 a.m.	37
Thursday, February 21	1:13 p.m.	36
Thursday, March 27	4:37 p.m.	35
Wednesday, April 30	1:47 p.m.	34
Tuesday, June 3	3:02 p.m.	34
Monday, July 7	3:26 p.m.	34
Sunday, August 10	10:40 a.m.	34
Saturday, September 13	12:45 p m.	34
Friday, October 17	11:54 a.m.	34
Thursday, November 20	10:40 a.m.	34
Friday, December 24	1:55 p.m.	34
1885		
Tuesday, January 27	1:17 p.m.	34
Monday, March 2	2:44 p.m.	34
Sunday, April 5	2:35 p.m.	34
Saturday, May 9	2:14 p.m.	34
Friday, June 13	1:56 p.m.	34

Date	Time of day	Days Out
1885 (continued)		
Thursday, July 16	4:30 p.m.	34
Wednesday, August 19	1:56 p.m.	34
Tuesday, September 22	1:19 p.m.	34
Monday, October 26	2:25 p.m.	34
Friday, November 29	2:05 p.m.	34
1886		
Saturday, January 2	3:16 p.m.	34
Sunday, February 7	3:28 p.m.	36
Sunday, March 14	3:25 p.m.	35
Saturday, April 17	2:41 p.m.	34
Friday, May 21	2:55 p.m.	34
Thursday, June 24	4:09 p.m.	34
Wednesday, July 28	3:48 p.m.	34
Tuesday, August 31	3:05 p.m.	34
Monday, October 4	2:05 p.m.	34
Sunday, November 7	2:46 p.m.	34
Saturday, December 11	1:29 p.m.	34
1887		
Monday, January 17	4:09 p.m.	37
Tuesday, February 22	2:40 p.m.	36
Tuesday, March 29	3:37 p.m.	35
Sunday, May 1	2:34 p.m.	34
Saturday, June 4	3:30 p.m.	34
Thursday, July 14	7:37 p.m.	40
Monday, August 22	10:45 a.m.	39
Monday, September 26	1:31 p.m.	35
Monday, October 31	1:47 p.m.	35
Monday, December 5	12:30 p.m.	35
1888		
Tuesday, January 10	2:29 p.m.	36
Thursday, February 16	1:55 p.m.	37
Monday, March 26	2:49 p.m.	39
Wednesday, May 2	3:05 p.m.	37
Thursday, June 7	11:14 a.m.	36
Sunday, July 15	9:48 p.m.	38
Wednesday, August 22	9:10 p.m.	38
Saturday, September 29	1:15 p.m.	38
Tuesday, November 6	11:45 a.m.	38
Wednesday, December 12	12:55 p.m.	36
1889		
Saturday, January 19	12:25 p.m.	38
Tuesday, February 26	1:20 p.m.	38

Deep River New Era, Friday, April 12, 1889

ESSEX

The beautiful lines in last week's *Era* on the Old Leather Man suggest to us the project of raising money in the different towns through which he tramped, to procure a suitable memorial to mark his lonely grave on the banks of the Hudson.

Stamford Weekly Advocate, Friday, April 12, 1889, Stanwich

The leather suit, which was worn by the "leather man," weighs 66 pounds. It is now on exhibition in the post office window at Sing Sing. He made his first trip through Stanwich during the month of May, 1856.

Bristol Weekly Press, Thursday, April 18, 1889

H. N. Gale recently came across an excellent photograph of the old leather man, in Hartford. He retouched it some and improved it so that it will satisfy his customers, many of whom have been looking about for a good likeness of the old chap.

Photographs of the "Old Leather Man" are for sale by H. N. Gale.

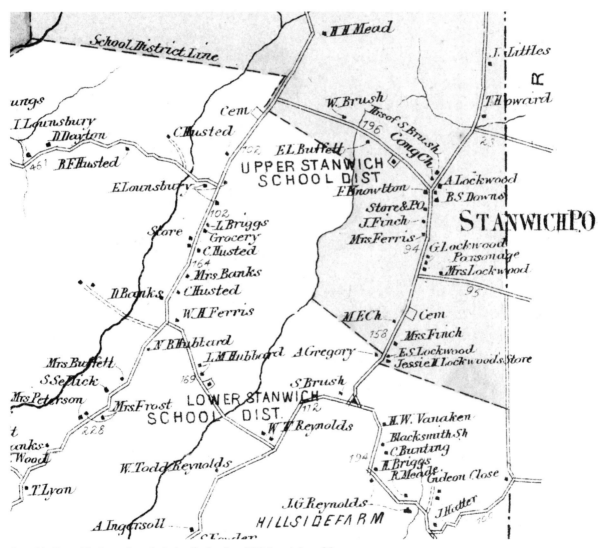

Stanwich, Greenwich, Connecticut. *Author's collection, from F. W. Beers Atlas, 1862.*

The Old Leather Man. Photograph taken in 1888 by F. W. Moore of Middletown and retouched by H. N. Gale of Bristol.

Penny Press, Friday, May 3, 1889

The Old Leather Man

In the cold, chilly winter, in the hottest summer
   weather,
In the daylight, in the moonlight, came the old man
   clad in leather;
In the storm, in the sunshine, at the hour he surely
   came.
Ever silent, not a murmur, never telling you his
   name.

But his journey now is over, we shall see his face no
   more.
He has crossed the swelling Jordan, safely landed
   on the shore;
He has changed his leather garments, for a robe as
   white as snow,
And is telling o'er his story, of his hardships here
   below.

How he lov'd a pretty maiden, how he courted, how
   he won
How their hearts were knit together, until they
   became as one;
Of the sacred vows they uttered, while the tears,
   like April showers,
Glisten'd in her eyes so dewy, like rich pearl drops
   'mong the flowers.

How he traded with her father, till there came a
   crash of fortune,
How they robbed him, drove him from her, ending
   all their happy courting;
Rent those two fond hearts asunder, nor would
   cease their cruel anger,
Till an ocean rolled between them, leaving him
   alone to wander.

Clad in garments made of leather, all alone the
   livelong day,
Till at night he found a shelter, in the wild woods
   far away;
Where the fern its fragrant plumage droops; or
   mossy covered hedge
Laid the old man down to slumber, among the
   leaves beneath the ledge.

There, like Jacob, saw a ladder, far from Heaven
   reaching near,
Saw descending the fair maiden, love had made to
   him so dear;
All night long she sat beside him, whispering words
   his heart to cheer,
Precious dream, richer, sweeter, than can come to
   millionaire.

"Come with me, ascend the ladder," said the sweet
   voice bright and clear,
"It will bring you to our Saviour, come with me,
   there's naught to fear;
Leave that body, clothed in leather, open not those
   eyes again,
Till you open them in Heaven, free from sorrow,
   free from pain."

So, together, they ascend, far away from mortal
   sight,
Till sweet music, song of Angels, thrill'd their souls
   with new delight;
Soon they reach the "golden city," soon the
   Heavenly host they scan,
Lo! the pearly gate swings open, "Welcome,
   Welcome, Leather Man."
   L. DIBBLE[9]
   Saybrook.

Cover of the booklet published by the Globe Museum; reproduced from an original

After the Leather Man died, his suit was put on display in John L. Birdsall's cigar store in Ossining. Then his suit and other paraphernalia were secured by Meehan & Wilson's Globe Museum at 298 Bowery Street in New York. The museum exhibited a life-sized figure of the Leather Man and published an accompanying booklet, titled "Life of the Mysterious Leather Man, the Wandering Hermit of Connecticut and New York," by A. B. Stewart. Later, the suit went on tour through New York and Connecticut. In February 1892 Soby's Cigar Store in Hartford displayed the clothes in its window. The Eden Wax Musée on Coney Island also exhibited the Old Leather Man's suit, which may then have been incinerated in the fire that destroyed the museum in 1928.

9. Linus Dibble.

LIFE OF THE
MYSTERIOUS LEATHER MAN

THE "OLD LEATHER MAN."
From POLICE GAZETTE, New York, Richard K. Fox, Prop.

THE
Wandering Hermit ⅋ Connecticut & New York.
GLOBE MUSEUM 298 BOWERY, N. Y.,
MEEHAN & WILSON, Proprietors.

From the Globe Museum booklet. Leroy W. Foote collection.

**Life of the Mysterious Leather Man, The
Wandering Hermit of Connecticut and New York
On Exhibitions at Meehan & Wilson's Globe
Museum, 298 Bowery, New York.
Written by A. B. Stewart, Lecturer
Examine the Contents.
New York:
New York Popular Publishing Co.
37 Bond Street**

PREFACE FROM THE BOOKLET

So much has been said and written within the last few years about the "Old Leather Man" that Messrs. Meehan and Wilson, the proprietors of the Globe Museum, 298 Bowery, New York, have on several occasions tried by generous offers to induce the old man to give up his tiresome self-imposed tramps, and to exhibit himself before that museum's patrons. All efforts in that direc-

tion, however, proved futile. But when a few months ago, death stopped the old man's wanderings; the next step was taken, and with flattering success. His odd suit of leather, well-worn by him over thirty-years, as well as other curious paraphernalia were secured through the kindness of George H. Sutton, coroner of Westchester County, and a life-size figure, an artistic reproduction of every feature of this wonderful old man was made, and clothed with the original leather apparel, for the museum a remarkable, realistic, life-like exhibit of the Old Leather Man.

It is the unselfish intention of the proprietors of the Globe Museum, Messrs. Meehan and Wilson, after their patrons have been offered a sufficient opportunity of viewing this interesting counterpart of the Mysterious Leather Man, to present the figure in its entirety to the Connecticut Humane Society, who have always displayed such a praise-worthy interest in the unfortunate Poor Old Leather Man.

A. B. Stewart

Invoice for the Old Leather Man's burial charges on March 25, 1889.

Citizen Register, Monday, May 18, 1953

More Than 60 See Unveiling
Of Plaque For Leather Man

More than 60 local residents and representatives of historical societies witnessed the unveiling Saturday of a bronze plaque in Sparta Cemetery marking the grave of the Leather Man, who toured the area between the Connecticut and Hudson Rivers from 1858–1889.

"The name on the plaque, Jules Bourglay, has not been determined absolutely to be that of the Leather Man," the gathering was told by LeRoy W. Foote of Middlebury, Conn. "It is the one that appears in contemporary records, however, and more than 400 people who knew the wanderer have affirmed this name to be correct."

Efforts to trace this and similar names in records of Lyons, the French city from which the traveler is supposed to have come, have been unavailing to date, said Allison Albee of Rye, a trustee of the Westchester County Historical Society

SEVERAL STORIES CIRCULATED

"Several stories were circulated to account for the leather-garbed vagabond who wandered the area for more than 40 years," Mr. Albee continued. "He was described as a murderer, as a veteran of the Napoleanic wars, and as a man, who failed as a leather merchant, the business of his sweetheart's father."

The Leather Man was well known in this part of the country, Mr. Albee pointed out, noting that his obituary appeared on the front pages of several New York newspapers. He was found dead in 1889 in a cave north of Old Chappaqau Road, between what is now Route 100 and the present Putnam Division tracks.

"The cave was destroyed when Gordon Road was widened three or four years ago," the Rev. Robert B. Pattison, pastor emeritus of the First Baptist Church, explained to a reporter after the ceremony. "I visited it several years ago, however, as part of the study for the Ossining Historical Society.

CUSTODIAN OF CEMETERY

The Ossining group currently is custodian of the historic Sparta Cemetery, in which several soldiers of the American Revolution are buried, Mr. Pattison said in opening the unveiling ceremony. The group took over responsibility for the burying ground several years ago from the First Presbyterian Church, its original trustee, he explained.

"My interest in Sparta Cemetery began when I discovered how many of my ancestors are buried here," said Elliot Baldwin Hunt of 64 Sherwood Avenue, president of the Westchester County Historical Society. "I believe that Hunt graves outnumber those of members of other old Ossining families buried here." The grave of the Leather Man is located in what was originally the pauper's section, just inside the gate at the intersection of Revolutionary and Albany Post Roads. Until last week, it was unmarked.

Introduced as donor of the plaque, Thomas J. Price of Astoria, Queens, indicated that credit should be shared with two County residents who wished to remain anonymous. He said he became interested in such items of Westchester history as the story of the Leather Man while residing in the Dunwoodie section of Yonkers several years ago.

INTRIGUES HISTORIANS

This bit of folklore has intrigued several historians, said Mr. Foote, introduced as authority on the Leather Man for Connecticut groups. The late Charles A. Beard investigated the wanderer's history, he said, and a Hart-

(Original newspaper caption.) *Unveiling monument in Sparta Cemetery to the Leather Man, who traveled area from Connecticut to Hudson Rivers from 1858 to 1889, is Jessica Ward Redway, daughter of Mr. and Mrs. George F. Redway of Ossining. More than sixty persons, including representatives of historical societies, attended the ceremonies near Ossining on Saturday morning. —Staff Photo. Leroy W. Foote collection.*

ford museum displays a leather bag carried by the wanderer and several implements believed to have been made by him which were found in Connecticut caves.

Displayed before the ceremony were several photographs of the Leather Man, in most of which he is shown holding his hand over his mouth. It was indicated that this gesture was affected to conceal a disfigurement caused by cancer of the lip, believed to have been the cause of his death.

Unveiling ceremony was performed by Jessica Ward Redway, nine-year-old daughter of Mr. and Mrs. George F. Redway of Noel Drive. Reflecting her Girl Scout training, Jessica took care that the folded flag covering the plaque did not touch the ground as she removed it.

DESCENDENT OF HUGENOT

Jessica's performance of the ceremony, in addition to the presence of the French tricolor beside the Stars and Stripes, accented the national origin of the Leather Man. She was introduced as a descendent of Isaac Coutant, one of the band of Hugenots who founded New Rochelle.

After the ceremony, as participants exchanged stories of the Leather Man told them by old timers, a bouquet predominantly of buttercups and pansies was placed on the grave by five-year-old Marsha Thompson, granddaughter of Mrs. C. L. Cormier of 76 Revolutionary Road. Marsha said she had picked the flowers herself.

The plaque was mounted upon a used granite headstone and placed near the iron pipe that had marked the grave for sixty-four years. Photo by D. W. DeLuca, 2000.

Appendixes

Artifacts and Portraits

COLLECTION OF THE CONNECTICUT HISTORICAL SOCIETY MUSEUM,
HARTFORD, CONNECTICUT

*The Old Leather Man's large leather bag.
Courtesy of the Connecticut Historical
Society Museum, Hartford, Connecticut.*

*The Old Leather Man's mitten. Courtesy of the Connecticut Historical
Society Museum, Hartford, Connecticut.*

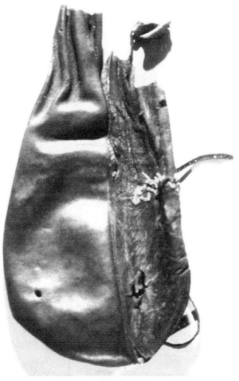

*The Old Leather Man's tobacco pouch. Courtesy of the Connecticut
Historical Society Museum, Hartford, Connecticut.*

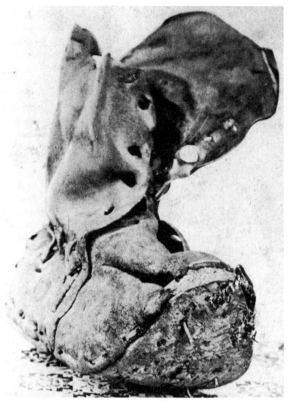

The Old Leather Man's hatchet, found in the dugaway cave/rock shelter in Woodbury, Connecticut, by Albert Barnes and given to Leroy W. Foote. The handle is about 14 inches long, and the blade about 9¼ inches by 1¾ inches. Leroy W. Foote collection.

This knife is located at the Connecticut Historical Society Museum. It may be a replica of the original knife that belonged to the Old Leather Man, because a replica was made by Leroy W. Foote and donated by his wife to the Connecticut Historical Society in 1985. Courtesy of the Connecticut Historical Society Museum, Hartford, Connecticut.

Photograph of the Old Leather Man's boot. Courtesy of the Connecticut Historical Society Museum, Hartford, Connecticut.

COLLECTION OF THE HAMDEN (CONNECTICUT) HISTORICAL SOCIETY

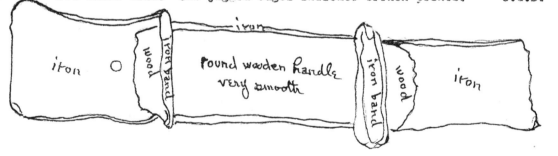

Sketch made by Carolyn G. Dickerman in 1948 of the Old Leather Man's knife, which was donated by J. Walter Basset to the Hamden Historical Society. Courtesy of the Hamden Historical Society.

This knife is located at the Hamden Historical Society. It is not known if it is the original knife. Collection of the Connecticut Historical Society Museum, Hartford, Connecticut.

One of many of the Old Leather Man's pipes left in his shelters. This pipe, with a tin bowl and oak stem, was found by Henry C. Dunham in a shack on his property in Maromas, Middletown, Connecticut. Courtesy of the Middlesex County Historical Society.

PHOTOGRAPHS IN THE AUTHOR'S COLLECTION

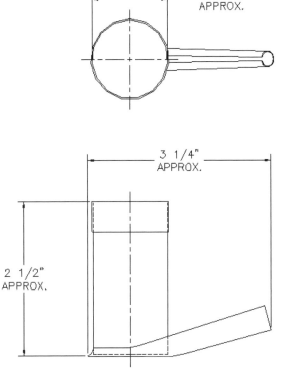

The Old Leather Man's boot; present location unknown. The soles of his boots were made from spruce wood that was about three fourths of an inch thick, and the leather tops were fastened to them with fifteen-gauge wire, formed like staples and a half inch in width, making them look like stitching. Leroy W. Foote collection.

Drawing of the Old Leather Man's pipe showing approximate dimensions. This pipe was made from two pieces of tin, most likely from a tin can. Drawing by Tracey Despres, scaled to the quarter inch. Courtesy of the Despres family.

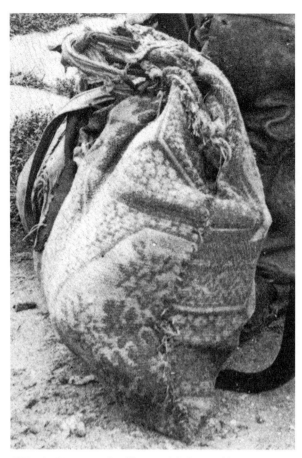

Old Leather Man's carpet bag (from a period photograph);
present location unknown.

L. M. Wool painted The Old Leather Man for John M. Crampton,
former Connecticut State Fish and Game Commissioner and president
and treasurer of the John M. Crampton Co., Inc., window shade
manufacturers at 671 Chapel Street, New Haven, Connecticut. The
painting (7′7″ by 27″) was displayed for many years at the top of the
stairs at Mr. Crampton's business and is now in the collection of Sheri
Kroll. Photo by D. W. DeLuca; courtesy of Sheri Kroll.

The Old Leather Man, by A. V. Durant. In 1892, Frank Knight
commissioned artist A. V. Durant to paint a nearly life-sized
(5′5″ by 3′11″) portrait of the Leather Man for the Nutshell Saloon in
East Derby, Connecticut. Durant based his painting on F. J. Moore's 1888
photograph that was retouched by photographer H. N. Gale. Today the
painting hangs in the Derby Public Library. Photo by D. W. DeLuca;
painting in the collection of the Derby (Connecticut) Public
Library, courtesy of the Derby Public Library.

APPENDIX B

Towns through Which the Leather Man Walked at One Time

CONNECTICUT
New Fairfield, Ball's Pond (shelter)
Danbury (shelter)
New Milford (shelter)
Bridgewater (shelter)
Bethlehem
Roxbury (shelter)
Waterbury (shelter)
Woodbury (tannery and four shelters)
Watertown (shelter)
Waterbury (shelter)
Middlebury (shelter)
Southbury (shelter)
Wolcott (shelter)
Oxford (shelter)
Naugatuck (shelter)
Goshen (shelter)
New Preston (shelter)
Thomaston (shelter)
Plymouth (shelter)
Harwinton (shelter)
New Hartford, Satan's Kingdom (shelter)
Burlington (two shelters, one named Tory's Den)
Wigville (Burlington)
Polkville (Bristol)
Forestville (Bristol)
East Bristol (shelter)
Plainville, Redstone Hill (shelter)
Morris (shelter)
Litchfield (shelter)
Torrington (shelter)
Winchester (shelter)
Newtown (shelter)
Canaan (shelter)
Bristol, Compounce (shelter)
Southington, East Street (shelter)
Berlin, Short Mountain (shelter)
Meriden (bottom of West Peek shelter)
Wallingford
Berlin, Four Rod Road (shelter)
East Berlin
Middletown, Westfield
Mount Higby, Middletown (shelter)

Middletown, Amy Guy residence (photo sessions)
Middletown, Fisher residence (photo sessions)
Middletown (shelter)
Durham (shelter)
Haddam, Higganum
Haddam (shelter)
Shailerville, Haddam
Tylerville, Haddam
Chester (food, doctor, shelter)
Killingworth (shelter)
Saybrook, Deep River (shelter)
Essex, Centerbrook (shelter)
Essex (shelter)
Old Say Brook
Westbrook (shelter)
Clinton (shelter)
Madison (shelter)
Guilford
Guilford, Leete's Island (shelter)
Branford (food, photo sessions)
East Haven (shelter)
North Haven
Hamden (shelter)
Woodbridge (shelter near Chamberlain's Shack)
Orange (shelter)
Milford, Naugatuck Junction railroad tower
Stratford (shelter)
Trumbull
Stepney (shelter)
North Bridgeport (shelter)
Weston (shelter)
Westport
Redding (shelter)
Wilton (shelter)
Norwalk (shelter)
New Canaan (shelter)
Long Ridge (shelter)
Hunting Ridge (shelter)
Greenwich, Sandwich
Greenwich, Audubon
North Greenwich (shelter)

NEW YORK: WESTCHESTER, PUTNAM, DUTCHESS, COLUMBIA, AND RENSSELA COUNTIES
Purdy Station
Rye (shelter)
Mamaronack (shelter)
Armonk (shelter)
Harrison (shelter)
Scarsdale (shelter)
White Plains (shelter)
Bedford (shelter)
Pound-Ridge (shelter)
Chappaqua (shelter)
North Salem (shelter)
Brewster, southeast (shelter)
Kensico (Mt. Kisco)
Bedford Hills (shelter at Bull Hill)
Croton Falls (shelter)
Doanesville
Yonkers (shelter)
Peekskill (shelter)
Ossining, Sparta Cemetery (grave)
Mt. Pleasant, Ryder Farm (shelter)
Mt. Pleasant, Dell Farm (two shelters)
Yorktown, Turkey Mountain (shelter)
Loyola (shelter)
Yorktown, Shrub Oak (shelter)
Jefferson Valley
Somers (shelter)
Baldwin's Place Station
Mahopac Station
Brewster Station

THE LEATHER MAN IS ALSO SAID TO HAVE TRAVELED INTO THE BERKSHIRES AND CANADA.

Selected Old Leather Man Sites Accessible to the Public

Many of the Old Leather Man's cave/rock shelters have been documented, and lists, maps, and photographs have been made and lost over time. I am presently working with others to compile a list (with maps and photographs) of locations for some of his shelters and eating places. The following is a preliminary list. For more information search the internet for "Leatherman's Circuit," Geocaching.

CONNECTICUT

Burlington: Tory's Den. This cave/rock shelter was used by the local Tories in Revolutionary times as a hiding place. Take East Plymouth Road off Route 72 in Harwinton, Connecticut, to the Tunxis Trail, opposite a sign reading "Old Marsh Nature Trails." Follow the trail for about a half mile to the junction of Tory's Den Trail and Mile of Ledges Trail. Follow the trail another half mile to Tory's Den. There is another of the Old Leather Man's cave/rock shelters about 150 feet east of Tory's Den.

Greenwich: Greenwich Audubon Center is located at 613 Rivesville Road in Greenwich. A map is available at the Center. The cave is off the Beach Hill Trail.

Hamden: Fann's Shelter. Owned by the Hamden Historical Society. Check with the society before going to the cave/rock shelter, located off Joyce Road in Hamden.

Meriden: Hubbard Park. Follow the path to the bridge going over 691 and up the hill to a wooden bridge on the left. Go over the bridge and up the hill to a stone bee hive spring. Take a left and follow the path, staying to your right. Just below the radio tower near the base of the cliff you will see the Old Leather Man's shelter.

Meriden: Mount Higby. The shelter is located north of Preston Notch on the east side of Mount Higby, near the old plane crash.

Watertown: two shelters. Follow the Mattatuck Trail crossing Route 6 in Watertown east to Crane Lookout, about one mile. The Rock House is on the south side of Crane Lookout. To get to the other cave/rock shelter follow the Jericho Trail south about two hundred yards to reach the overhanging Jericho Rock in Thomaston.

NEW YORK

Armonk: Helicker's shelter. West of Route 22, behind the Old Armonk Bowl.

Briarcliff Manor. The shelter is located on Hillcrest Drive, about one hundred yards past the dead-end sign, on the right, next to the road, under a large slab rock. This shelter is on the Old Ryder Farm near the Old Dell Farm where the Leather Man died.

Cross River: Ward Pound Ridge Reservation. Go to the Trailside Museum for directions to the cave. The museum has a Leather Man display and also offers occasional talks and guided tours to the cave.

Ossining. The Old Leather Man's grave is in Sparta Cemetery, off of Route 9 going south. The entrance is on Revolutionary Road, and the grave is in the way back to the right off to the side, just three feet from a stone column. Stop in the Ossining Historical Society for more information.

Annotated Bibliography

LITERATURE

Albee, Allison. *The Leather Man.* Westchester Historical Society, 1937.

Brunvand, Jan Harold. *The Vanishing Hitchhiker: Legends and their Meanings.* W. W. Norton, 1981.

Clyne, Patricia Edwards. *Caves for Kids.* Library Research Associates, Inc., 1992. See especially chapter 3: "Lair of the Leatherman."

Develin, Dora Harvey Munyon. *A Life for a Life and Other Stories.* Published by F. Tennyson Neely, 1899. Contains a little tragedy called "The Faithful Lover." This is the story of Jules Bougereau, the son of a poor lumber merchant in Paris, and of Marie Le Rue, daughter of Pierre Le Rue, a wealthy leather dealer of noble blood. Jules and Marie loved each other, but Monsieur Le Rue would not hear of their marriage. However, he finally agreed to take Jules into his business and to give them his consent if, within a year, Jules had proved himself worthy of trust and confidence; if not, Jules was to disappear from Paris. Before the year was up, the Le Rue mansion was destroyed by fire, and Monsieur Le Rue perished in the flames. Marie became very ill from the shock and soon after died. Following the funeral, Jules wandered aimlessly about and finally disappeared.

Dorson, Richard M., ed. *Handbook of American Folklore.* Indiana University Press, 1983.

Gackenback, Dick. *The Leatherman.* Seabury Press, 1977. A children's book of a fictionalized boy's encounter with the Leatherman.

Grant, Steve. "In the Footsteps of the Leatherman." *Hartford Courant,* 1993. A thirteen-part series by a *Courant* reporter.

Johnson, Foster Macy. *The Romantic Legend of Jules Bourglay, the Old Leather Man.* Bayberry Hill Press, 1977. A fictionalized tale based on some documented incidents of his life in Connecticut and New York.

Mohr, Charles E., and Howard N. Stoan, eds. *Celebrated American Caves.* Rutgers University Press, 1955. See esp. Leroy W. Foote's chapter: "The Leatherman."

Philips, David E. *Legendary Connecticut: Traditional Tales from the Nutmeg State.* Curbstone Press, 1992.

Smith, Bertram R. A. *History Repeated.* Old Saybrook Press, 1982. A collection of stories, one of which is entitled "Leatherman Country."

Snow, Charles Wilbert. *The Selected Poems of Wilbert Snow.* Stephen Dayne Press, 1936. See esp. "The Leather Man," pp. 94–99.

Stewart, A. B. *Life of the Mysterious Leather Man, the Wandering Hermit of Connecticut and New York.* Meehan & Wilson's Globe Museum, 1889

AUDIO AND VIDEO

Kachuba, Mike. *It Happened In Connecticut.* CD. Acoustic Traditions Music, 2004.

McKeon, Edward Jr. *The Road between Heaven and Hell: The Last Circuits of the Leatherman.* Television documentary. International Television Association, 1984. Sketches the life of the Old Leather Man and offers some explanation for his actions and for why his life story still fascinates people today.

Pearl Jam. "Given To Fly." Sony Music, 1998. The B-side to the CD single contains a song called "Leatherman," words/music by Eddie Vedder.

Sullivan, George. *Walkie in the Parlor.* CD. Folkway Records, 1947. The song entitled "The Leatherman" had been passed down from generation to generation, and George Sullivan sang it to Evelyne Beers in 1945. Folkway Records recorded Sullivan around 1947. The Smithsonian Institution acquired Folkways in 1987 to ensure that the label's preservation. Smithsonian Institution, Folkways Cassette Series 02376.

Additional Resources

Branford Library and Historical Society, the James Blackstone Memorial Library, 758 Main Street, Branford, CT 06405, (203) 488-1441; The Harrison House, 124 Main Street, Box 504, Branford, CT 06405, (203) 488-4828, www .branfordhistory.org/contact.html

Connecticut Historical Society Museum, 1 Elizabeth Street at Asylum Avenue, Hartford, CT 06105, (860) 236-5621, www.chs.org/visiting.htm, email: ask_us@chs.org

Connecticut State Library, 231 Capitol Avenue, Hartford, CT 06106, (860) 757-6500, www.cslib.org/

Guilford Library and Historical Society, 67 Park Street, Guilford CT 06437, (203) 453-8282, www.gulfordfreelibrary.org/

Hamden Historical Society Library, Miller Memorial Cultural Center, 2901 Dixwell Avenue, Hamden, CT 06518, hhs@hamdenlibrary.org, email joepepel@comcast.net

Middlesex Historical Society, 131 Main Street, Middleton, CT 06457

Ossining Historical Society, 196 Croton Avenue, Ossining, NY 10562, (914) 941-0001, info@ossinonghistorical.org

Watertown Historical Society, 22 Deforest Street, Watertown, CT 06795, (860) 274-1050, watertownctmuseum@sbcglobal .net

Ward Pound Ridge Reservation, in Cross River, New York, (914) 864-7317

Westchester County Historical Society (Library and Research Center), 2199 Saw Mill River Road, Elmsford, NY 10523, (914) 592-4323, www.westchesterhistory.com/

Index

Page numbers in italics indicate illustrations; page numbers in bold indicate maps. OLM is used as an abbreviation of Old Leather Man in index entries.

Garnet Books

Titles with asterisks (*) are also in the Driftless Connecticut Series

Garnet Poems: An Anthology of Connecticut
   Poetry Since 1776*
   Dennis Barone, editor
The Connecticut Prison Association and the
   Search for Reformative Justice*
   Gordon Bates
Food for the Dead: On the Trail of New
   England's Vampires
   Michael E. Bell
The Long Journeys Home: The Repatriations
   of Henry 'Ōpūkaha'ia and Albert Afraid
   of Hawk*
   Nick Bellantoni
Sol LeWitt: A Life of Ideas*
   Lary Bloom
The Case of the Piglet's Paternity: Trials from
   the New Haven Colony,1639–1663*
   Jon C. Blue
Early Connecticut Silver, 1700–1840
   Peter Bohan and
   Philip Hammerslough
The Connecticut River: A Photographic
   Journey through the Heart of New
   England
   Al Braden
Tempest-Tossed: The Spirit of Isabella Beecher
   Hooker
   Susan Campbell
Connecticut's Fife & Drum Tradition*
   James Clark
Sunken Garden Poetry, 1992–2011
   Brad Davis, editor
Rare Light: J. Alden Weir in Windham,
   Connecticut, 1882–1919
   Anne E. Dawson, editor
The Old Leather Man: Historical Accounts of
   a Connecticut and New York Legend
   Dan W. DeLuca, editor
Paved Roads & Public Money: Connecticut
   Transportation in the Age of Internal
   Combustion*
   Richard DeLuca
Post Roads & Iron Horses: Transportation in
   Connecticut from Colonial Times to the
   Age of Steam*
   Richard DeLuca
The Log Books: Connecticut's Slave Trade
   and Human Memory*
   Anne Farrow

Birding in Connecticut*
   Frank Gallo
Dr. Mel's Connecticut Climate Book
   Dr. Mel Goldstein
Forever Seeing New Beauties: The Forgotten
   Impressionist Mary Rogers Williams*
   Eve M. Kahn
Hidden in Plain Sight: A Deep Traveler
   Explores Connecticut
   David K. Leff
Maple Sugaring: Keeping It Real in
   New England
   David K. Leff
Becoming Tom Thumb: Charles Stratton,
   P. T. Barnum, and the Dawn of American
   Celebrity*
   Eric D. Lehman
Homegrown Terror: Benedict Arnold and the
   Burning of New London*
   Eric D. Lehman
The Traprock Landscapes of New England*
   Peter M. LeTourneau and
   Robert Pagini
Westover School: Giving Girls a Place of
   Their Own
   Laurie Lisle
Heroes for All Time: Connecticut's Civil War
   Soldiers Tell Their Stories*
   Dione Longley and Buck Zaidel
The Listeners: U-boat Hunters During the
   Great War
   Roy R. Manstan
Along the Valley Line: A History of the
   Connecticut Valley Railroad*
   Max R. Miller
Crowbar Governor: The Life and Times of
   Morgan Gardner Bulkeley*
   Kevin Murphy
Fly Fishing in Connecticut: A Guide for
   Beginners
   Kevin Murphy
Water for Hartford: The Story of the Hartford
   Water Works and the Metropolitan
   District Commission
   Kevin Murphy
African American Connecticut Explored
   Elizabeth J. Normen, editor
Henry Austin: In Every Variety of
   Architectural Style
   James F. O'Gorman

Breakfast at O'Rourke's: New Cuisine from a
   Classic American Diner
   Brian O'Rourke
Ella Grasso: Connecticut's Pioneering
   Governor*
   Jon E. Purmont
The British Raid on Essex: The Forgotten
   Battle of the War of 1812*
   Jerry Roberts
Making Freedom: The Extraordinary Life of
   Venture Smith
   Chandler B. Saint and
   George Krimsky
Under the Dark Sky: Life in the
   Thames River Basin
   Steven G. Smith
Welcome to Wesleyan: Campus Buildings
   Leslie Starr
Barns of Connecticut
   Markham Starr
Gervase Wheeler: A British Architect in
   America, 1847–1860*
   Renée Tribert and
   James F. O'Gorman
Forgotten Voices: The Hidden History of a
   Connecticut Meetinghouse
   Carolyn Wakeman
Connecticut in the American Civil War:
   Slavery, Sacrifice, and Survival
   Matthew Warshauer
Inside Connecticut and the Civil War: One
   State's Struggles*
   Matthew Warshauer, editor
Connecticut Architecture: Stories of 100 Places
   Christopher Wigren, Connecticut
   Trust for Historic Preservation
Prudence Crandall's Legacy: The Fight for
   Equality in the 1830s, Dred Scott, and
   Brown v. Board of Education*
   Donald E. Williams Jr.
Riverview Hospital for Children and Youth: A
   Culture of Promise*
   Richard Wiseman
Stories in Stone: How Geology Influenced
   Connecticut History and Culture
   Jelle Zeilinga de Boer
New Haven's Sentinels: The Art and Science
   of East Rock and West Rock*
   Jelle Zeilinga de Boer and
   John Wareham

About the Driftless Connecticut Series

The Driftless Connecticut Series is a publication award program established in 2010 to recognize excellent books with a Connecticut focus or written by a Connecticut author. To be eligible, the book must have a Connecticut topic or setting or an author must have been born in Connecticut or have been a legal resident of Connecticut for at least three years.

The Driftless Connecticut Series is funded by the Beatrice Fox Auerbach Foundation Fund at the Hartford Foundation for Public Giving. For more information and a complete list of books in the Driftless Connecticut Series, please visit us online at http://www.wesleyan.edu/wespress/driftless.